TEAM MINISTRY

Putting together a team that makes churches grow

By Dick Iverson
— with Ray Grant —

For pastors, Christian leaders, teachers,
church planters, and students of church growth

TEAM MINISTRY

captures twenty years of actual experience
in church growth...and church planting work...
condensed and packed into one volume

EIGHT BASIC PRINCIPLES

One: Identifies the problems which bind most churches and prevent them from growing spiritually or numerically--no matter what their size, 100-500-700-1000, 2000 or even 3000.

Two: Reviews the traditional forms of church government and considers how the principles of team ministry can be utilized in your congregation.

Three: Examines the Biblical precedents for team ministry in the Old Testament.

Four: Analyzes the New Testament definition of ministry and the principles of team ministry as were utilized in the early church.

Five: Evaluates the various ways in which your church will benefit by adapting team ministry principles.

Six: Presents the guidelines which the author proposes for setting up a team ministry in your church.

Seven: Sets forth how to maintain the long-range benefits of team ministry by prayerfully watching over twelve areas of practical relationships.

Eight: Shows how to train new elders to form a growing and outreaching leadership team.

"Must reading for teachers and students as well as pastors and Christian leaders involved in church planting ministries."

BIBLE TEMPLE PUBLISHING TITLES BY DICK IVERSON

PRESENT DAY TRUTHS
MAINTAINING BALANCE
THE HOLY SPIRIT TODAY
RESTORING THE CHURCH
RESTORING THE FAMIILY

RELEVANT ISSUE BOOKLETS

AVOIDING BURNOUT
THE SABBATH PRINCIPLE
SPIRITUAL AUTHORITY
THE FEAR OF GOD
BEING A PROPHETIC PEOPLE
TODAY'S PROPHETS
REPENTANCE

TEAM MINISTRY

TO

MY WIFE EDIE

and my four daughters

Debi, Diane

Brenda, and Tracey

AND TO

THE ELDERS OF

BIBLE TEMPLE

without whose support this

book would not have been possible.

ACKNOWLEDGEMENTS

I wish to express my appreciation to Ray Grant for helping me develop this book, which is based upon a series of lectures given at various Pastors Seminars, and working with me in completing this manuscript. Ray has been associated with me at Bible Temple for nearly twenty years and has witnessed how team ministry works. I also want to thank Roxy Kidder for transcribing the recorded messages and her good work in typing the original manuscript.

I also wish to express my appreciation to Harry Albus for the labor of love he has given to the production of this book. He has put valuable time and energy as well as his vast experience into editing the manuscript and marketing of this book because he believes in its message. Without his help and encouragement, I doubt if you would be reading this. I also want to thank his wife, Isla, for the hours she has given in typing and proofreading the finished manuscript.

Pastor Dick Iverson

TEAM MINISTRY

Putting together a team that makes churches grow

By Dick Iverson
—with Ray Grant—

BIBLE TEMPLE PUBLISHING
Portland, Oregon

Unless otherwise identified, all Scripture references are from the King James Version of the Bible.

Library of Congress cataloging in Publication Data
Iverson, Dick

Team Ministry
ISBN 0-914936-61-1

CONTENTS

CONTENTS

CONTENTS

FOREWORD

It is a real pleasure to be able to write a Foreword to the new edition of TEAM MINISTRY. This is so for two special reasons: firstly, because of about ten years of ministerial association with Bible Temple, and secondly, because we were part of the "team ministry" in Bible Temple and saw the principles of TEAM MINISTRY in operation over these years.

With regard to TEAM MINISTRY, I believe the following comments will be helpful.

It is to be remembered that there is no (as yet) "perfect church." However, the Lord has given to every Bible believing church certain deposits which belong in and to the Body of Christ as a whole.

All churches are not to be compared with, nor are they "Bible Temple" churches, nor do they have the "chemistry" of Bible Temple.

However, over the years, in every church where I personally have ministered, I have endeavored to learn from them as well as minister to them.

We are not speaking about the "mechanics" of church life, for "the letter (only) kills but the Spirit gives life." But we do seek for Biblical principles of the Word and Spirit that will work in any church, in any nation and in any culture.

As this book is read and studied, various statements and propositions will impress different ministers and their leadership, and will also be applicable in their distinct local church situations. However, these same statements can be used or misused. They can be a blessing to some, or, through misinterpretation and misapplication can create problems in others.

In traveling ministry, through observation and discussion, I have found two particular extremes, and these concern the role of the senior minister, and the role of the plurality of eldership.

Some leaders have taken statements from this book and used them to rationalize absolute plurality of eldership and stifle any senior man from taking leadership responsibility. Other leaders have taken things from this same textbook and made the senior man the sole authority and the eldership a group of "yes-men." Both become extremes and must be avoided.

This is why an earlier paragraph said that the same statements in this book can be used or misused, and can be a blessing to some, but through misinterpretation and misapplication can create problems for others.

Balance is absolutely necessary. We are all creatures of extremes, and we all have the tendency to use the part of the whole that suits us or our particular situation or problem.

In Numbers 27:16-17, Moses, a shepherd-leader, prayed that the Lord would *set a man over the congregation* that would go out before them and go in before them, that the congregation be not as sheep without a shepherd.

There must be a "set man," whether he be apostle, prophet, evangelist, pastor or teacher, and whether he be called senior minister, senior pastor, or whatever!

There must be a helmsman at the helm of the ship or those on board may suffer shipwreck.

There must be a driver of the bus. There must be the "angelos" of the church. There must be the "set man." The "set man" works with others, an eldership, a plurality of men who, together, are "checks and balances" for each other.

We see this pattern in both Old and New Testaments.

* Moses and the elders - Exodus 4:29
* Joshua and the elders - Joshua 7:6
* Samuel and the elders - I Samuel 15:30
* David and the elders - I Chronicles 11:3
* Solomon and the elders - I Kings 8:1,3
* Peter and the apostles - Acts 2:14
* James and the elders - Acts 21:18
* Paul and the elders - Acts 20:17-33
* Christ and the 24 elders - Revelation 5:6

Thus, the Old Testament and the New Testament set forth the pattern of "the set man" who takes the lead, and "the elders" who together lead the people of God.

This book should be read and studied in the light of these things so that leadership may receive the blessings of the principles it intended to set forth.

We pray that those who read, study and use TEAM MINISTRY will also see the Lord for the spirit and principles of life behind the letter of this text.

Kevin J. Conner
Senior Minister
Waverley Christian Fellowship
Melbourne, Australia

PREFACE   *Why I had to write this book*

Our church sponsors an annual Pastors' Conference which draws pastors and Christian leaders from all over the nation and some foreign countries. In addition, it is my privilege to speak to a variety of Pastors' Conferences and Seminars each year.

People seem to be impressed by the fact that our church has put together a team ministry concept that works and has maintained an annual growth pattern of twenty to twenty-five percent. And so they come from everywhere to see if they can discover for themselves, as one pastor put it, "What makes you tick."

"That's all very well for churches your size," many have said to me, "but we're little guys compared to you. We still have to get our first one hundred people."

Tell me about it. I was still in my twenties when my wife and I worked with my father in a church which was founded with only thirteen people. We saw that group grow to 150 people by the time my father resigned for health reasons and the pastorate was turned over to me.

"But look what happened to you," some have said, "while we've been on a plateau for years."

We've been there, too. For the first four years we remained on a plateau and were fast headed for extinction. Every time some major problem or emergency developed, I began to feel that the Lord was trying to tell me something. Perhaps He was calling me to be an evangelist.

"What did you do? How did you get off the plateau?" they ask.

Well a lot of changes took place, mostly in two areas. First, a wave of revival came our way and the Lord opened up our eyes to see many new principles in the meaning of praise and worship. Second, in the practical area, we had to learn that it was more important to build a family then to draw a crowd.

"How did you get to that point?" they ask.

Today, pastors from all over the nation keep telling me about their problems. To spell out a few:

"In our church while some are coming in the front door, others are going out the back door."

"I have some in my church that want me to run everything. Others want me just to give the sermon."

"I have to do everything in my church, even the janitorial work," some say.

"I haven't had a complete vacation in years. Whenever I do go, someone is always calling me back to marry or bury someone," is a recurring problem.

"Why should we build a new church now when Jesus is coming soon?"

Over and over again, I've heard it all, many times.

Among other things, I did what the merchants tell you to do when they sell you something:

When all else fails read the directions.

It took a while, but it finally got through to me that as a pastor that meant, *going back to the Bible.* It told me what to do practically, as well as spiritually.

1. What should we do about the problems pastors and church leaders face? It's in the Bible.

2. How should we apply God's Word to the various church management problems we confront? It's in the Bible.

3. The Old Testament reminded me--that it takes more than one man to run a ship, build a kingdom or a city, or even the temple of God.

4. The New Testament "directions" or ministries...the fivefold ministry in leadership...and how the saints are equipped to minister...astonished me.

I couldn't believe what I was reading! It was all there...in the Bible. It's been there for centuries. Waiting to be discovered.

As I began putting these "directions" into practice, I experienced a second wave of shock -- *the benefits were enormous, beyond belief.*

The directions really worked!

So when I heard pastors from everywhere crying for help, I began to hear the Lord say in my heart, "Feed my sheep and my shepherds."

That's why I had to write this book. I had to see if I could help some of the shepherds who may need help as much as I needed help especially in the early years of my ministry.

The other part of the story--the spiritual development, the growth of the worship experience--that phase of my story, which I believe is one of the most important factors in getting our church off of its plateau, will have to be left to another book.

In this volume, I hold as carefully as possible to one theme: *the building of team ministries in the body and the management of that body through team ministry so that all parts (or members) of the body minister to one another.*

Included also in this book are guidelines for developing team ministry in your church, maintaining the long range benefits of team ministry, and training new elders to form the leadership team of the future.

One more word: read in this book what I have discovered in over thirty years of ministry. I have tried to present it as faithfully and honestly as I can. I found it in the Bible and have tried to put it into practice. *It works.*

I believe beyond a doubt that if you also put it into practice, it will work for you, too. All you have to do is check it out for yourself from the primary source--THE BIBLE--and then follow the directions.

Dick Iverson, Senior Pastor
Bible Temple, Portland, Oregon

PART ONE

The pastor's dilemma in a growing church

Some of the subjects discussed:
- The beginnings
- Suddenly our church came alive
- The stranger in our house
- Controlling everything from the pulpit
- A family versus a crowd
- The shepherd and his associates
- Indispensable but not indestructible
- The eschatological problem
- The ambidextrous superperformer
- Then, there is the first family

If you have ever seen a husband try to solve the dilemma of a growing family all by himself (or a wife try to do it all by herself), you have some idea of how a pastor or Christian leader goes wrong when he tries to solve local church problems by himself.

It takes a team to be really successful. In a marriage, it takes husbands to love their wives and wives who are loving help-meets to their husbands. It takes both of them. Working, praying, and growing together. Submitting to one another (Ephesians 5:21).

Administering the problems of local churches successfully--especially growing churches--makes team ministry virtually mandatory.

When team ministry is developed and perfected in local church administration, almost any growth goal is attainable. The sky is the limit!

That's what this book is all about. How to build a team ministry that enables churches to grow, and grow, and grow...perhaps even to astronomical sizes heretofore thought impossible, but increasingly desirable in an urban society.

In my early years

I co-pastored for ten years before becoming a senior pastor in 1961. At this writing, I have been pastoring that church for nearly thirty years.

I was raised in a very traditional Pentecostal environment and took over the church from my father when his health broke down in the late fifties. My wife and I did our best to pastor the church in the way we were taught. It was, basically in our tradition, the way everybody did it in those days. Things went okay. Nothing spectacular. But we didn't have much fruit those first five years.

PASTOR'S DILEMMA

The beginnings of growth

In our fifth year, 1965, the Lord blessed our church body in a sovereign way. And growth began to take place. We were very excited about this growth after experiencing five frustrating years of stagnation. In a small community, it seems sometimes that you don't have many fish to gather. But when you're in a large metropolis and people are everywhere, it is more or less assumed that you should have some kind of growth process.

Suddenly our church came alive

What a thrill it is, after five arduous years of laboring without any growth, to suddenly experience a church body coming alive.

God was moving sovereignly. A beautiful spirit and strong worship permeated our meetings. Exceptional changes took place. The church not only came alive. It began blossoming out. This sudden growth took place just before the "Jesus Movement" and the "Charismatic Movement" in the United States. From that point on, our growth increased steadily by twenty to twenty-five percent annually.

And then, almost as suddenly, we were thrust into a new dilemma: *the crisis of success.* Until that time we had not thought of success in relation to crisis. But that is what it can become, if one doesn't know how to handle it.

The stranger in our house

We came to a time in the growth of our church when the attendance moved upward steadily...from 200 to 300, then to 400 and on and on until it reached 700. Suddenly, I discovered that the stranger in our house was not only the visitors or members but the pastor. I got so I didn't dare ask people how long they had been coming to church, or where they came from.. Because if I did I might be embarrassed when they replied: "We've been coming here

TEAM MINISTRY

for a couple of years, pastor."

Believe it or not, that was what was beginning to happen! I didn't know the people. I didn't know their children. And sometimes I didn't know what was going on. But what I did know was that something was wrong, seriously wrong.

Controlling everything from the pulpit

If growth continued, I would soon be controlling everything from the pulpit. A situation I wanted to avoid, since I was keenly aware of the results of such a ministry in the history of the church. Concentration on a pulpit ministry too often meant controlling a congregation from the pulpit on Sunday mornings. But what other option was there? There were so many people. So many needs. Those who helped me in those days automatically served in a subservient role. Meanwhile I continued to shoulder the increasingly large burden of the ministry. The distasteful role of a pulpiteer was thrust upon me more and more.

A family versus a crowd

My desire was to build a Christian family relationship. Not draw a crowd of spectators. Many eloquent speakers can muster a crowd. Many churches can draw people and hold their interest through Sunday school contests, bike races, kite flying, etc. But the result is--attracting crowds, not building a personal, intimate family.

The parable of the shepherd

I became aware of the words of Jesus in the parable of the shepherd and his flock in John 10. The more I read these words, the more frustrated and guilty I felt.

But he that entereth in by the door is the shepherd of the sheep. To him the porter openeth; and the sheep hear his voice; and he calleth his own sheep by name, and leadeth them out. And when he putteth

PASTOR'S DILEMMA

forth his own sheep, he goeth before them, and the sheep follow him: for they know his voice. (John 10:2-4)

I began to hunger for that kind of personal relationship with all the sheep that God had entrusted into my care. But the glaring impossibility of it overwhelmed me. I staggered emotionally. And wondered when this guilt-trap would snap and engulf me totally.

The shepherd and his associates

Not comprehending the importance of other ministries in a local church setting, I treated my associates in traditional fashion. When assistants came into the church, I related to them as boss and hirelings.

My attitude seemed to say, I'm the boss and you are my assistants. When I tell you to jump, you are supposed to ask, how high. I would tell them what to do, snap my fingers, and then they would perform! I hasten to say that I had good men, powerful men, gracious and submissive people who had joined themselves to me. But the extent of my leadership was to tell everybody what to do. And then make sure they did it. What's more, when they didn't do it right, I would step in and do their task for them.

The commander in chief

I was running the ministry like an army. Like a coach of a football team. Or, in a hardhanded business approach. One person in charge of this. Another in charge of that. And a hierarchy of command. In a growing church that was constantly moving ahead, I was responsible for everything. Every decision had to come to my desk. Every project had to be okayed in my office. And every task had to be closely supervised.

Indispensable, but not indestructible

If I went on a vacation I had to call home every day to

make sure everything was running smoothly. I couldn't relax while on vacation because an emergency might arise, and I might have to rush home. Then, as always, someone usually needed marrying or burying. The subliminal concept that dominated my thinking was "this church cannot operate without me."

Finally, all the activities, and all the necessary things in which a minister is supposed to be involved, brought me to the end of myself, physically! I was showing some physical changes in my body that I didn't like. My usual therapy--relaxing vacations--was insufficient. I came to the place where I wasn't going to make it unless there were some drastic changes. I was pacing the floor on sleepless nights. Physically, mentally, and emotionally, I was drained. Something had to change. That was my dilemma.

The eschatological problem

This was another undercurrent which dominated my leadership style that influenced the way the church was going. It was the idea that I only had today in which to work. This idea caused me to overextend myself to the point of exhaustion. Jesus is coming soon. We don't have very many days left. The end is just around the corner, or over the hill, so don't worry about fifty years from now. Or, even twenty-five years from now. Or, even ten years from now. Why? Because Jesus is coming soon.

This was the eschatological emphasis and expectancy when I was a teenager. And when the atom bomb went off, it became magnified. They told me it was just a matter of time. This earth is going to melt in fervent heat. And that would be it!

As a fifteen-year-old boy, when the bomb went off, I no longer had time for tomorrow. I was told I didn't have time to spend several years in a Bible college. Nor to prepare for the ministry. I was encouraged to take off at the age of nineteen and get to the job of winning the world for Christ.

Needless to say, I quickly came to a place of deep frustration, principally because I didn't have adequate preparation for such a task as winning the whole world within a few years or months.

In addition, it became a rude awakening to discover that people weren't eagerly awaiting my arrival. It took fifteen years of self-learning that I might have largely assimilated within a couple of years had I taken the time to sit at the feet of experienced godly teachers.

It was this mentality: that Jesus is coming tomorrow, that you must hurry and get the job done--even if you have to do it all by yourself--that can quickly destroy a ministry for all its good intentions. It leads to personal exhaustion, and a spirit of frustration at best. And to burnout if not to experience complete physical or nervous breakdown at worst.

Dealing with great expectations

All men like to have the respect of their friends. They all desire to live up to the expectation that others have for them. Pastors are no different. They would like to be able to live up to the expectations of the members of the congregation. The problem is that sheep sometimes expect a lot out of their shepherd. And they tend to murmur and complain when these desired characteristics are not all forth-coming.

The ambidextrous superperformer

I have already mentioned that a pastor needs to know his sheep personally. But a long list of other requirements follows.

TEAM MINISTRY

The pastor must be:
Instantly available for crisis counselling
Provide assistance during emergencies
Train his people for ministry
Settle interpersonal problems
Maintain discipline
Provide guidance counselling
Admonish and exhort the weary and brokenhearted
Do the work of evangelism
Visit new "prospects"
Officiate at funerals, weddings, baptisms, dedications
Maintain public relations with the community
Administrate departments efficiently
At times balance the budget
Do janitorial work and maintenance repairs
And, let's not forget driving the bus

To accomplish all of these feats successfully and always appear to be perfectly calm, relaxed and even tempered would require the combined talents of a superman and a wonderwoman plus the ambidextrous physical properties of an octopus.

Then, there is the first family

This is an additional expectation that definitely must be fulfilled if all of the sheep are to be kept happy. The pastor must exhibit an exemplary family life. The pastor's family is constantly on display. The church expects his family to be a spotless, prim and proper example. Amidst the abundance of other duties, the pastor has to find time for his own personal prayer life, Bible study, and grooming, as well as, caring for the personal needs of his lovely wife and patient children.

I have seen many pastors struggle between caring adequately for their own family, and fulfilling the duties of the ministry. Often the family is sacrificed mercilessly in the name of God and ministry. Some ministers fail to realize the family is ministry! They are "winning the world, but losing their own family."

Husbands, love your wives, even as Christ also loved the church, and gave Himself for it...fathers, provoke not your children to wrath: but bring them up in the nurture and admonition of the Lord. (Ephesians 5:25; 6:4)

Leaving hollow monuments

I hope to live another fifteen or twenty years before I leave planet earth although no one actually knows his departure time. When that time comes, I would like to think that my life had not been spent in vain. That whatever else I did, I laid a good foundation for the next generation.

Will the thirty years of involvement--which has been my life---all of a sudden come to a screeching halt?

Will my church fall apart, split, divide, disband, and leave behind a big building as a hollow monument to the days when Dick Iverson, Senior Pastor, was there?

There is no happiness in thinking about such a future for the people sitting in a big monument in which nothing is happening. And only the hollow sounds of faded memories are echoing through the walls, if indeed, even that were forthcoming. So that, too, is one of the dilemmas facing a pastor of a growing church.

Building a work that lasts

I do not like to think of building a work of God that does not last, even beyond my years. It is inconceivable to think about fruit that does not remain. God says he is interested in fruit that remains:

...I have chosen you, and ordained you, that ye should go and bring forth fruit, and that your fruit should remain...(John 15:16)

TEAM MINISTRY

Now I would really love to have the Lord return soon, just as you would. But if He doesn't, I want to lay a foundation in my life and my ministry upon which my successors will continue to build. My hope would be that they would even excel the work that was completed during my lifetime.

I would love to have them look back to the days when I was on the scene and say "those were good days." But there is something better than that, that they will continue to say "but these are greater days" and "there are greater days still ahead of us."

Why? Because Dick Iverson, Senior Pastor, laid a good foundation.

That's what I've been working on these thirty years. Not only to build a team ministry to solve the multitudinous dilemmas that face all pastors and church leaders of growing churches. But also to build a work that when I pass from the scene, I will leave *lasting footprints on the sands of time.*

PART TWO

Applying God's Word to church government

with brief reviews of
five traditional forms

When we consider the area of ministry and Christian leadership in a local church, we are dealing with more than the natural man. We are confronting the spiritual man.

Consequently, it can no longer be our primary objective to solve our problems solely on a human level. We must look for solutions that reach into the supernatural realm.

We need also to remind ourselves that the church has to do with Jesus Christ, who said, "...I will build My church; and the gates of hell shall not prevail against it" (Matthew 16:18). So when we come to solving the problems of church government, we are touching on more than a human organization, although human beings are involved. We are also dealing with a spiritual organism.

Church government, therefore, has to do with both a human organization and a spiritual organism. The latter being the body of Christ, made up of people who are miraculously born into the kingdom of God through regeneration (John 3:3).

Three streams flowing through Christendom

Not long ago I was at a conference where there were ministers from all different denominations of Protestantism and Roman Catholicism. One of the speakers made the statement that what he saw happening in the world of today was, as it were, like three streams flowing through Christendom.

PASTOR'S DILEMMA

One of the great streams which the Evangelical people had kept flowing, he said, was the doctrine of the redemptive work of the cross, that is, salvation by faith alone. The second stream which he envisioned was the stream of the spiritual gifts and the empowerment of the Holy Spirit. This stream had been maintained by the Pentecostals and Charismatics. Then he startled the conference by saying that the third stream that had been kept flowing in a pure state was a specific denominational system and its government of the church.

These three streams are going to come together and flow as one, he predicted.

Now, I don't know what that does to you, but that statement sent shock waves up and down my spine. Anyone with an elementary grasp of reality knows that whoever controls the government of the church controls the whole spectrum of church life, including its ministry.

This is why we say that church government is very important. It is important because the ministry of the church is so closely related to church government. In my opinion, there is only one way to evaluate and properly control the government of the church. And that way is found in Jesus Christ, who is in Himself--THE WAY, THE TRUTH, and THE LIFE (John 14:6). Our information on how Christ is to govern His church is found in God's Holy Word.

Applying God's perspective

When we deal with the ministry of a local church we must approach the matter with utmost sincerity. We do not consider the matter superficially. We must scrutinize and evaluate any concept of ministry under the full light of God's Word.

Our perspective, our way of looking at the concept of ministry, must be from God's viewpoint. Our vision must be from God's perspective.

TEAM MINISTRY

Human perspectives will fail. Traditional perspectives will fall short. Only God's perspective will produce life in the church and in the earth. The primary source for obtaining light on God's perspective is in the Word of God.

For My thoughts are not your thoughts, neither are your ways My ways, saith the Lord. For as the heavens are higher than the earth, so are My ways higher than your ways, and My thoughts than your thoughts.

For as the rain cometh down, and the snow from heaven, and returneth not thither, but watereth the earth, and maketh it bring forth and bud, that it may give seed to the sower, and bread to the eater: so shall My word be that goeth forth out of My mouth: it shall not return unto Me void, but it shall accomplish that which I please, and it shall prosper in the thing whereto I sent it. (Isaiah 55:8-11).

Consider the traditional forms of government

Basically, there are five different forms of church government. There may be smaller variations of these five forms, but for our purposes, a brief review of each of these five should be adequate.

I. ONE-MAN RULE

The form that is found in most independent churches is the one-man rule. At the risk of being oversimplistic, we might say that he is the supreme ruler, benevolent despot. He makes all the decisions. He alone sets the goals and the people are encouraged to accept his "indispensable" autocratic authority. He is the source of enthusiasm, of new ideas, and of programs. This "untouchable" lordliness is referred to in the words of Christ:

...Ye know that they which are accounted to rule over the Gentiles exercise lordship over them; and their great ones exercise authority upon them.

But so shall it not be among you: but whosoever will be great among you, shall be your minister: and whosoever of you will be the chiefest, shall be servant of all. (Mark 10:42-44)

CHURCH GOVERNMENT

Weak at best...Dangerous at the worst

We know that at best this is a relatively weak form of government. At worst, it is dangerous. As a one-man leadership goes so goes the church. The temptations that accompany this form are legion. This position of prominence, with its autocratic power to form church policy, and its freedom from restrictions, can cause even the strongest saint to forget the admonition of Paul:

> For I say...to every man that is among you, not to think of himself more highly than he ought to think; but to think soberly, according as God hath dealt to every man the measure of faith.
>
> For as we have many members in one body, and all members have not the same office, so we, being many, are one body in Christ, and every one members one of another. (Romans 12:3-5)

A "boss" mentality most always insures disaster. And when the minister shipwrecks, the people are washed ashore in an agony of distress. Some do not even survive the waters of bitterness. I have lived long enough to watch this happen many times in our land. It is very sad.

A tragic example

There was a great church in one of the large cities of America during the late forties which experienced a mighty move of God. For years the church was packed to the doors every single night. This revival was one of the key moves of God in our nation. Many will testify that "God was there," in the beginning. It was such a sovereign act of God that almost every pastor in the city visited those meetings sooner or later.

But then it became controlled by man's methods and man's ways. Extremes and imbalance took place. Fanaticism and improper use of money followed. And eventually, the leader shipwrecked in several areas of his life. When he went down, guess what happened to the church? It became a reproach to the whole city.

TEAM MINISTRY

Untouchable but not infallible

As I look back on it, I recall that this pastor was "untouchable." He acted alone and he stood alone. But he did not suffer alone.

Confusion and hurt overtook the city for years. Independent churches everywhere suffered because of the poor reputation of that one independent church. I know that all of us have seen and felt the heartache of people who have suffered under a person who has no checks and balances, who runs well for a while, then shipwrecks and brings a great work down in ruin.

In this type of church government, as well as in all of the others, everything is okay when there are no problems at hand--in a day of peace. Government is not that vital when everything is peaceful. But when the storms come--not if the storms come, but when--then according to the strength of that foundation so shall the house stand or fall. That is why a solid and lasting concept of ministry is so important. That is why it is necessary to seek the Lord.

> *He that heareth, and doeth not, is like a man that without a foundation built an house upon the earth; against which the stream did beat vehemently, and immediately it fell; and the ruin of that house was great. (Luke 6:49)*

II. CONGREGATIONAL FORM OF GOVERNMENT

This is the second form of church government, sometimes called the "people's party." It is usually an unlimited democracy. The people vote to move benches, paint buildings, hire or fire preachers.

The minister has no ruling power beyond that which he has as a regular member of the church. He is simply hired to teach and preach and administer the religious rites and sacraments. This "popular" form of government makes the ministry entirely dependent upon the will and action of the people.

Someone has said that the danger of this form is that the pastor has a tendency to take a poll before he writes his sermon, instead of proclaiming "Thus saith the Lord."

I hasten to say that this clearly is not true in all congregational churches, yet the potential is frightening.

Historical examples

The secular history of the ancient Greek city-states shows the glaring reality of the failure of an unlimited democratic form of government. That may be why the founders of the United States insisted upon a republican democracy and thereby insure a more stable and tranquil future.

The history of the Israelites was jeopardized continually by their "popular" democratic urges. From the day they left Egypt, the "voice of the people" was at variance with "the men of God" who were chosen by God to lead them. It culminated in their cry to be rid of God's ministers (or judges), end the theocracy, and by popular demand, adopt a monarchy as did the pagan nations.

> And the Lord said unto Samuel, Hearken unto the voice of the people in all that they say unto thee: for they have not rejected thee, but they have rejected Me, that I should not reign over them. According to all the works which they have done since the day that I brought them up out of Egypt even unto this day, wherewith they have forsaken Me...now therefore hearken unto their voice...(I Samuel 8:7-9)

Rejected ministers

Many a minister has labored diligently and with great sacrifice to himself and his family for years, only to find himself out in the street at a sudden whim of a congregational mood.

Ministers, with their wives and children, have been shuttled around the country as an annual affair because the local people have tired of them. This hardly seems a way to honor those "who labor in the Word and doctrine" (I Timothy 5:17).

TEAM MINISTRY

The result: preachers' kids are some of the most bitter individuals in society; the emotional drain on dedicated wives is heartbreaking; and the discouragement rampant in rejected ministers, who have been voted out of office, is beyond description.

The benefits of autonomy

There is a good word, however, for this congregational type of government. That is in their dedication to the autonomy of the local church, as opposed to outside control by a foreign governing body.

III. BOARD OR COUNCIL CONTROL

The third form of government found in churches is the trustee or deacon board control. In general, this consists of a council of prominent members, or a group consisting of businessmen, who among other things, hire and fire the pastor. The trustees usually are elected for a term from the general membership of the congregation. Since one of their duties is to keep the pastor in line, so to speak, they do add a dimension of checks and balances to a church which is totally absent in a one-man government.

The trustees make the major decisions for the church, manage much of the administration, and determine the feasibility of programs and projects in the church. The role of the pastor is usually confined to perform religious rites and to preach on Sundays. He is controlled and answerable to the board or council.

Sometimes the men on the trustee board are called elders. But the elders are businessmen, primarily; not spiritual elders or ordained ministers.

IV. CENTRAL OR EXTERNAL CONTROL

This is the fourth type of church government. In this form a church is externally controlled by a regional or national headquarters, or some particular external organization. This external control may be the state, as in some European countries; an order of bishops, independent and self-perpetuating; or supreme pontiff; or a denominational headquarters.

When there are problems, the external organization has authority over the local church, usually because they own the property. They can come in and remove the pastor, boot out the board, or do whatever they want to do.

V. ELDERSHIP MANAGEMENT

The fifth form of local church government is eldership management. Here, several ministers (spiritual elders) work in shepherding the congregation of the local church. Together, as a team, they minister to the people whom God has set into the local body.

This form of government could be termed team ministry. And because I believe this is a Biblical form of local church government--and of church ministry (we previously stated that the two are vitally linked)--we ought to seek out its principles and implications further.

The Bible gives God's perspective on this matter. From our viewpoint, the Bible is the only approach we can take if we are able to build upon a solid foundation. The Word of the Lord is our guide in doctrine and in practice.

Now he that planteth and he that watereth are one...for we are labourers together with God: ye are God's husbandry, ye are God's building. According to the grace of God which is given unto me, as a wise masterbuilder, I have laid the foundation, and another buildeth thereon. But let every man take heed how he buildeth thereupon. For other foundations can no man lay than that is laid, which is Jesus Christ. (I Corinthians 3:8-11)

PART THREE

Examining Old Testament patterns of team ministry

- In the beginning
- Three examples from Moses
- Consider the parable of the trees
- Discovering **team ministry**
- Look at the rebuilding of Jerusalem
- The value of counsellors
- The benefits of the threefold cord

We have looked at the pastor's dilemma in a growing (or non-growing) church. And we have applied the perspective of God's Word to a brief review of five traditional forms of church government.

Now, before we being our study of the New Testament patterns of team ministry, let us examine some of the principles that God established in the Old Testament.

The Apostle Paul taught that the realities that we enjoy in the spiritual realm were first typified and demonstrated in the natural realm:

> *For the invisible things of Him from the creation of the world are clearly seen, being understood by the things that are made, even His eternal power and Godhead...(Romans 1:20)*
> *Howbeit that was not first which is spiritual, but that which is natural; and afterward that which is spiritual. (I Corinthians 15:46)*

Many of the principles of God, the spiritual principles, can be made clear by the natural things of life. What then does the Old Testament reveal about team ministries?

In the beginning, the family unit

God established the family unit by creating Adam and Eve. We might label them plural parents. It is possible today for a single person to have a family, barely. But for complete fulfillment you need a couple to have a complete family. It is God's design that a person not try to have a family alone. God has ordained that a man have a wife, or a woman have a husband. And that as a team they function as a family unit.

OLD TESTAMENT PATTERNS

It seems reasonable that if God ordained a team ministry in the small family unit where decision making involves only a small number of people, then beyond doubt he would ordain team ministry in the house of God. Just as the wife is to function with her husband as a co-leader in the family, so elders are to function with the senior pastor as co-laborers in the church family.

This co-leadership does not in any way detract from the concept of headship. Team ministry can function in an atmosphere of recognition of the roles of each member. The wife can serve as a co-leader of the family and fully acknowledge the headship of her husband. The elders can likewise serve as co-leaders in the church and fully acknowledge the headship of the senior pastor.

Three examples from Moses

There are three instances in the life of Moses, while he was leading the people of God out of bondage, that pertain to the principle we are studying. The first is when Moses was given Aaron to help him approach the Pharaoh:

> And he shall be thy spokesman unto the people...he shall be to thee instead of a mouth, and thou shalt be to him instead of God. (Exodus 4:16)

Moses recognized his limitation in natural abilities, to the extent of angering God. Another man was allowed to complement him, and supply the talents which he lacked. Paul and Barnabas in the New Testament formed a good working team relationship in the same way (Acts 13:1-5).

Another instance is found when the burden of settling disputes as a judge became too heavy. Moses took the advice of his father-in-law, Jethro, and appointed others to help:

> ...Why sittest thou thyself alone, and all the people stand by thee from morning unto even?

TEAM MINISTRY

...Because the people come unto me to inquire of God.

The thing that thou doest is not good. Thou wilt surely wear away, both thou, and this people that is with thee: for this thing is too heavy for thee; thou are not able to perform it thyself alone. Hearken now unto my voice, I will give thee counsel, and God shall be with thee...and thou shalt teach them ordinances and laws, and shalt shew them the way wherein they must walk, and the work that they must do.

Moreover thou shalt provide out of all the people able men, such as fear God, men of truth, hating covetousness; and place such over them, to be rulers...(Exodus 18:14-21)

The third instance is recorded in Numbers. The spiritual burden of interceding for the people and trying to develop their character had overwhelmed Moses to the point of wanting to commit suicide.

God's answer was the appointing of seventy elders to stand beside Moses:

I am not able to bear all this people alone, because it is too heavy for me. And if Thou deal thus with me, kill me...

And the Lord said to Moses, Gather unto Me seventy men of the elders of Israel...and I will come down and talk with thee there: and I will take of the Spirit which is upon thee, and will put it upon them; and they shall bear the burden of the people with thee, that thou bear it not thyself alone. (Numbers 11:14-17)

How many ministers can relate to the frustrations of Moses? We pour out our very strength and soul in service to our congregations. We bear the burdens alone. Fight spiritual battles alone. Stand in the gap alone. And then come to the end of ourselves, weary of ministry and even of life.

God has a better way

God's solution is simple. You don't have to go it alone. Appoint, seek out, find able men: men of truth, hating covetousness, and fearing God. If Moses needed others to minister alongside him--the one who communicated with God face to face--we certainly are foolish to attempt to do the whole job alone. Perhaps God will also pour out his Spirit upon men whom we choose to help us, and they too will prophesy both within and without the camp (Numbers 11:25,29).

Consider the parable of the trees

There is a parable found in the book of Judges that is worth looking at:

> *The trees went forth...to anoint a king over them; and they said to the olive tree, Reign thou over us. But the olive tree said unto them, Should I leave my fatness, wherewith by me they honor God, and man, and go to be promoted over the trees?*
> *And the trees said to the fig tree, Come thou, and reign over us. But the fig tree said unto them, Should I forsake my sweetness, and my good fruit, and go to be promoted over the trees?*
> *Then said the trees unto the vine, Come thou, and reign over us. And the vine said unto them, Should I leave my wine, which cheereth God and man, and go to be promoted over the trees?*
> *Then said all the trees unto the bramble, Come thou, and reign over us. And the bramble said unto the trees, If in truth ye anoint me king over you, then come and put your trust in my shadow...(Judges 9:8-15)*

Permit me to lift this parable out of its historical setting and use it to illustrate a point of importance. All societies need leadership of some sort. Leadership is a requirement in the body of Christ.

Some individuals do not like the thought of someone being over them. But the Bible admonishes us to obey them that rule over you as they must give an account for your souls (Hebrews 13:17). And the trees here, which represent people, needed a ruler over them. They wanted someone to lead them. So they went forth to anoint a king over them.

Olive Tree. First they approached the olive tree. It refused. "Should I leave my great ministry and be involved with lowly people?" You see, the anointing oil came from the olive tree, so we might liken this tree to the great preacher-type ministry.

Fig Tree. The fig tree was asked next. It too refused. "Should I forsake my sweetness, and my good fruit, and be promoted over the trees?" Some ministries are more concerned about their own character gifts, their own personal tranquility and happiness which they have found in the quiet cloisters of their study, rather than being involved in the turmoil and turbulence of other people's character struggles.

The Vine. In desperation, the people then went to the vine. But the vine prefers its wine that brings cheeriness. This type of ministry majors in the joy of the Lord. The minister with the wine characteristic can go to a place and stir it up and bring the joy of the Lord.

The Bramble. The people continued their search. "Won't anyone care for us?" "Won't somebody come and lead us?" When they approached the bramble, it willingly obliged them. In Old Testament days, the bramble was used to make a fence around the sheepfold so the wild animals could not come in. Some pastors have the ministry of protection.

The whole point of this little parable, as I would like to apply it, is that while different individuals have different ministries, they all are needed in the local church. Instead of having the oil ministry (or the wine ministry, or the fruit ministry), they all can contribute on a "team basis" to the local assembly. A local church cannot get by with just a protection ministry. All of the ministries are needed in the church.

One-man ministries or single pastors need to realize that they do not have everything. The thought can be a remarkable discovery, or a rude awakening! We like to consider ourselves the "Shell answer man" for the whole body of believers. "If you have any problems, bring them

to my desk and with my great wisdom I will solve all of them."

Discovering team ministry

Until we discover the remarkable benefits of team ministry we will treat our ministry as supreme. And other types of ministries to the body as secondary. We will tell associates what to do. How to do it. And if they do not do it right, then we will do it all over again. After all, we tend to feel we can do it better anyway.

Somewhere, somehow, we must stop and analyze our concept of ministry. When we do, we may discover that the Biblical idea of team ministry recognizes the worth of all ministries.

Look again at the rebuilding of Jerusalem

We are all familiar with the great work that Nehemiah accomplished in rebuilding the city of Jerusalem and the temple. Look again and notice that he relied upon other strong men to lead the people along with them.

> ...I gave my brother Hanani, and Hananiah the ruler of the palace, charge over Jerusalem: for he was a faithful man, and feared God above many. (Nehemiah 7:2)

Notice the two qualifications that were listed: faithfulness, and the fear of God. Much can be accomplished when one is surrounded by faithful men who know they will give an account to God for everything with which they have been entrusted.

That team of faithful men was able to hold off an entire confederation of enemies. And that team also accomplished the restoration of God's people at Jerusalem. The evil forces engulfing local churches today make it mandatory for teams of faithful men to lead us today as was necessary yesterday.

TEAM MINISTRY

A wise man and his counsellors

Three times the book of Proverbs speaks of a multitude of counsellors:

> *Where no counsel is, the people fall: but in the multitude of counsellors there is safety. (Proverbs 11:14)*

> *Without counsel purposes are disappointed: but in the multitude of counsellors they are established. (Proverbs 15:22)*

> *For by wise counsel thou shalt make thy war: and in multitude of counsellors there is safety. (Proverbs 24:6)*

This wise king (Solomon) considered it of extreme importance to repeatedly mention the need for a multitude of counsellors. Can we today, as ministers, do otherwise? And go it alone, to keep the people from falling, to establish purposes, and to wage war? No! Safety comes where there is a team of counsellors.

The benefits of the threefold cord

King Solomon also recorded an interesting passage in Ecclesiastes on the value of a threefold cord.

> *Two are better than one; because they have a good reward for their labor. For if they fall, the one will lift up his fellow: but woe to him that is alone when he falleth; for he hath not another to help him up... And if one prevail against him, two shall withstand him; and a threefold cord is not quickly broken. (Ecclesiastes 4:9-12)*

What the Old Testament says

The message in the Old Testament seems to be loud and clear: team ministry.

We admit, of course, that church polity cannot be based on symbolism and parables. Nor on spiritualization of literal-historical passages in the Old Testament. But they do have value, as Paul stated, as types (representations, symbols of something to come) and as a basis for New Testament teachings.

So with this in mind, let us turn to the teachings of Jesus Christ and the apostles in the New Testament for a solid foundation of conduct and practice in managing local church government.

PART FOUR

Consider the
New Testament
definition of ministry

- Three groups are clearly defined
- Notice the variety of terms
- The danger in exclusiveness
- Several words describe ministers
- Watch those synonyms
- The fivefold ministry
- Consider how a home is managed
- Notice the plurality of elders
- The role of the senior elder
- The synagogue and the Jewish church

After many years of study as well as pastoral experience, I have come to the firm conclusion that the Biblical pattern for local church leadership and public ministry is team ministry.

In this section, we will look at the Biblical definition of ministry in the New Testament. We will consider the words used to describe church leadership and the number of leaders. Then we will take a new look at the role of the pastor so that you can evaluate for yourself whether my conclusion is a valid one.

Three groups are clearly defined

In the greeting in his letter to the Christians at Philippi, Paul addressed three groups of people: the saints, the bishops, and the deacons.

> *...the servants of Jesus Christ, to all the saints in Christ Jesus which are at Philippi, with the bishops and deacons. (Philippians 1:1)*

This introduction would seem to indicate that there are only these three groups of people in the house of God. (Notice that they are all mentioned in the plural.)

First, there are the saints

The saints are the gathering or congregation of all the believers in Philippi. This does not mean just a select few, who have been nominated to sainthood. But saints, here, refers to all the believers in the house of God.

Then, there are two offices

The other two groups mentioned by Paul are the two offices in the church: the office of the bishops, and the office of the deacons. The office of the deacons involves mainly the ordered service, meeting the social needs of the saints. Since it is not within the scope of the purpose of this study, we will not deal with this office at this time. Our purpose is to examine the word "bishops" as it pertains to ministry in general, and to team ministry in particular.

Notice the variety of terms

One of the problems we have in Christendom is that ministers have so many different titles. We have a conglomeration of terms to contend with when speaking of the ministry: cardinals, archbishops, bishops, presbyters, pastors, superintendents, elders, popes, canons, priests. As a result, there are a variety of positions which have formed, and a number of hierarchies which have developed.

However, note that in the Bible God often used many words to describe the same thing. For instance, He uses over seventy words to describe His church. He calls it an army, a city, the mountain of God, His bride, and so on. And if you get caught up in these different descriptions, you might--as some do--end up chopping the body into seventy different groups, each of which head off into its own little corner. We're of the bride company. We're of the overcomer company. We're of the army company. All of a sudden we have fragments all over Christendom.

The danger in exclusiveness

For example, those who are in "the bride company" corner

have an exclusive group because they have built their doctrinal stance on only a descriptive word about the church. They have limited their own perspective with God and their perspective and influence with people as well. It is always dangerous to our witness of Christ when there are exclusive groups in the body of Christ.

The same problem occurs when we deal with terms used to describe ministry. There are different words in the Greek, but they all describe the same ministry. For example, some will look at the word for ministry which is translated "bishop" and form a church government based on a hierarchy of bishops. Others will take another Greek word for ministry, like "elder" or "presbyter" and build a government based on one or the other. Still others zero in on the word "pastor" and establish churches with pastors as the form of church rule.

This problem can be overcome when we examine what these words in the Greek mean, and how they are used in their context.

Several words describe ministers

In the New Testament several words are used to describe ministers in the local church. Some of these were also common names for the ministers in the synagogues. "Wise men" as seen in Paul's request for a wise man in I Corinthians 6:5. "Leaders" was another name used when Judas and Silas are called "chief men among the brethren" (Acts 15:22).

Elder and Bishop. The term "elder" was one that the Jewish Christians were familiar with in connection with religious rulers. Elders stood alongside Moses (Numbers 11:16). Elders accompanied Joshua in conquest (Joshua 7:6). The Sanhedrin contained elders (Matthew 26:3), and the local synagogues were ruled by elders.

When the Jewish apostles wrote to local churches it

NEW TESTAMENT DEFINITION

was natural for them to address the elders. These were men who had an established position and who were recognized as having the oversight and responsibility for the pastoral care of their fellow-believers. They not only wrote about the elders, they referred to themselves as elders.

> *The elders which are among you I exhort, who am also an elder, and a witness of the sufferings of Christ, and also a partaker of the glory that shall be revealed: feed the flock of God which is among you, taking the oversight thereof. (I Peter 5:1-2)*
>
> *Is any sick among you? let him call for the elders of the church; and let them pray over him...(James 5:14)*
>
> *The elder unto the elect lady and her children, whom I love in the truth. (II John 1)*
>
> *The elder unto the wellbeloved Gaius, whom I love in the truth. (III John 1)*

In the writings of Peter, James and John, it is taken for granted that the office of elders is a well-known and acceptable institution.

The Greek word presbuteor translated here as "elder" simply means older, elder, or mature. It was not unnatural for the new churches in the New Covenant to retain, with some modification, the title for rulers that they are familiar with under the Old Covenant in the old synagogues.

Bishops. The word episkopoi is translated four times in the King James Version as "bishop" (Philippians 1:1; I Timothy 3:2; Titus 1:7; I Peter 2:25), and once as "overseer" (Acts 20:28). It was an official title among the Greeks designating commissioners appointed to rule new colonies. It has the connotation of ruling or overseeing.

Paul uses this word when writing to churches on Gentile soil. Philippi was in Macedonia. Timothy was located in Ephesus. Titus was in Crete. He seems to have accommodated his communication to the vernacular of the

TEAM MINISTRY

local people. But as we all see, he used it as a synonym for elders.

Watch those synonyms

To show clearly that the words "bishop" and "elder" both refer to the same man in the role of ministry, let us look at the fifth chapter of First Peter:

> *The elders which are among you I exhort, who am also an elder...feed the flock of God which is among you, taking the oversight thereof...(I Peter 5:1-2)*

Peter was an elder, writing to elders. But wasn't he also an apostle? Yes! He was both an elder and an apostle. "Elder" describes the man. "Apostle" describes his job or role in the ministry.

It is interesting to note how Peter wrote to elders: "who am also an elder." He seemed to be writing as an equal, and not someone superior.

The fivefold ministry

In the "fivefold ministry" (apostle, prophet, evangelist, pastor, teacher), I don't think the apostle is on the highest rung on the ladder, so to speak; nor is the prophet one step lower; nor the evangelist lower still. No, I see them as coequal, fellow-elders in the ministry, but with different roles.

There's no competition nor contention for a higher place in this hierarchy. This is where the strength of team ministry comes from. It is in the recognition of each other's roles in ministry.

Pastor. Peter continued by exhorting the elders to "feed the flock." This is the verb form of the Greek word "shepherd" or "pastor," poimen. It is translated both "feed" and "rule" as in Matthew 2:6, "out of thee shall come a

Governor, that shall rule (shepherd) My people Israel." Peter is using the concept of elders, and the role of pastoring, interchangeably.

Bishop. Then Peter added "taking the oversight thereof." Here is the verb form for "bishop." Peter not only used the concept of elders and pastors interchangeably, he also used all three concepts--elders, pastors, and bishops--to describe the same ministry. This truth is brought out again in the book of Titus:

> *For this cause left I thee in Crete, that thou shouldest set in order the things that are wanting, and ordain elders in every city...For a bishop must be blameless, as the steward of God...holding fast the faithful word as he hath been taught, that he may be able by sound doctrine both to exhort and to convince the gainsayers. (Titus 1:5,7,9)*

Here Paul talked about elders. Then halfway through his instructions he told Titus he was talking about bishops. It must be that the terms are synonymous, referring to the same ministry. And Paul added that these men must also be able to teach the people the Word (verse 9). This is tantamount to feeding the flock; that is, functioning in the role of pastor.

Luke recorded another incident in the life of Paul which reinforces this truth on the definition of ministry. Paul called for the elders of the church in Ephesus (Acts 20:17) and said:

> *Take heed therefore unto yourselves, and to all the flock, over the which the Holy Ghost hath made you overseers...(Acts 20:28)*

Again, all three concepts of ministry are present here: elders, watching over the flock (pastors); and overseeing (bishops); and the apparent implication is that they refer to the same ministers at Ephesus.

It is interesting to note that when Paul's writings containing the words for "bishop" were translated into the

TEAM MINISTRY

Aramaic for Hebrew Christians, the translators saw to it that this term was invariably rendered by *"kashisho"* (the Aramaic word for "elder"). The word "bishop" disappeared altogether from the Peshito, the oldest translation of the New Testament, in favor of "elder." The two words must indeed be synonymous.

Pastor. A few comments about the Greek word for pastor, *poimen.* In the New Testament this word is used eighteen times. Fifteen times it is translated "shepherd," especially in the Gospels. In two instances it refers to "the Great Shepherd and the Chief Shepherd" (Hebrews 13:20; I Peter 2:25). Only once is it translated "pastor" (Ephesians 4:11).

The verb form *poimaino,* is translated six times as "feed" and four times as "rule." Three of these ten times it has a definite reference to ministers "shepherding" the flock of God (John 21:16; Acts 20:28; I Peter 5:2). Four times it refers to Jesus Christ "ruling" in the earth as the Governor (Matthew 2:6), as a Lamb (Revelation 7:17), as a Male Child (Revelation 12:5), and as the Word of God (Revelation 19:15).

The words which we hear repeatedly in modern churches, "the pastor," and which are associated with a local church, were unknown in the early church. The word "pastor" is never used in reference to a minister of a church, only when it referred to Christ: the Chief Shepherd, the Great Shepherd, or the Good Shepherd. Primarily it seems that this terminology does not refer to the man, the person; but rather to the role of the person, that of shepherding God's people. Pastoring is just one of the five basic roles of ruling elders: apostles, prophets, evangelists, pastors, and teachers. Table 1, on page 39 shows the relationship of "pastor" (and the other fivefold ministries) to the words "bishop" and "elder."

NEW TESTAMENT DEFINITION

TABLE 1
RELATIONSHIP OF PASTORS AND FIVEFOLD MINISTRIES

BISHOPS	episkopoi	(means overseer)	Describes THE OFFICE
ELDERS	presbuteroi	(means older, mature)	Describes THE MAN
PASTORS	poimen	(means shepherd, rule)	Describes THE WORK (ROLE)
also APOSTLES	poimen	(means shepherd, rule)	THE WORK (ROLE)
PROPHETS	poimen	(means shepherd, rule)	THE WORK (ROLE)
EVANGELISTS	poimen	(means shepherd, rule)	THE WORK (ROLE)
TEACHERS	poimen	(means shepherd, rule)	THE WORK (ROLE)

Bishops and elders are broad, general terms that do not specify the particular type of ministry.

Apostle, prophet, evangelist, pastor and teacher are more specific, descriptive words for the type of ministry or work with which the ministers are involved. They tell how the mature men will oversee the people of God in the local church.

Consider how a home is managed

In the parental aspect of a home there are two people: the mother and the father. They are not in competition. They just have different roles. The same is true with the ministers who are apostles, prophets, or pastors, etc. They are not in competition with each other. But they harmoniously work together in overseeing different jobs in the church. Some teach. Some give strength. Some are seers. Some stir up the people in evangelism.

TEAM MINISTRY

It would be good here to emphasize that the elders were spiritual ministers, ordained ministers. They were men set apart for spiritual leadership in the body. They were not merely businessmen who controlled the church. They were not simply popular or prominent people in society. Instead, they were men called by God to one of the fivefold ministries. They may have supported themselves by secular occupations, such as Paul in tent-making or Peter in fishing, but they had a definite ministerial call on their lives.

Notice the plurality of elders

A glaring fact that jumps out as we read the Scriptures that deal with the early church is that there was more than one elder in a local church. There was a plurality of leadership. There were several individuals with certain powers and duties engaged in a common pursuit.

It was a team ministry where there was joint action by a group of elders, in which each person subordinated his individual interests and opinions to the unity and efficiency of the group. As peers, according to their ordained roles, all watched over the flock; not just one pastor, as is common today. The presbytery in a church was a group of spiritual elders who had oversight in the house of God (I Timothy 4:14).

Even though no set number is given, in relation to the New Testament local church, elder is used in the plural form. Throughout the book of Acts there is repeated reference to the elders (plural) when it speaks of the church and its ministers:

...The disciples...sent it to the elders (Acts 11:29-30)

And when they had ordained them elders in every church (Acts 14:23)

And when they were come...they were received...of the elders (Acts 15:4)

NEW TESTAMENT DEFINITION

Then pleased it the apostles and elders, with the whole church (Acts 15:22)

They delivered them the decrees...that were ordained...of the elders (Acts 16:4)

He sent to Ephesus, and called the elders of the church (Acts 20:17)

And all the elders were present (Acts 21:18)

The Epistles and the rest of the books also speak in the plural:

Let the elders that rule well be counted worthy (I Timothy 5:17)

Let him call for the elders of the church (James 5:14)

The elders which are among you I exhort (I Peter 5:1)

Thou shouldest set in order the things that are wanting, and ordain elders (Titus 1:5)

Remember them which have the rule over you (Hebrews 13:7)

Obey them that have the rule over you (Hebrews 13:17)

Salute all them that have the rule over you (Hebrews 13:24)

There are two exceptions in the Scriptures where the plural is not used. The first is I Timothy 3:2 and Titus 1:7, and when taken in its context it does not negate the idea of plurality. Here Paul is giving Timothy and Titus the list of qualifications that "an elder" or "a bishop" must have in order to be ordained, and join the group of elders in leadership. To show that this is the correct interpretation we need only recall that Timothy is at Ephesus at this time where there are known to be several elders (Acts 20:17). The second exception is found in II John 1 and III John 1 where the Apostle is beginning his letter with a salutation. He designates himself as "the elder." However, it is not logical to construe this as to mean John was a single elder in a local church, rather it points out the fact that he was a noted elder throughout the region.

TEAM MINISTRY

A beautiful example of team ministry is portrayed in the thirteenth chapter of Acts. Much good is said about the great church in Antioch, but this passage clearly refers to a team of ministering elders functioning in this local church:

> Now there were in the church that was at Antioch certain prophets and teachers; as Barnabas, and Simeon that was call Niger, and Lucius of Cyrene, and Manaen, which had been brought up with Herod the tetrarch, and Saul. (Acts 13:1)

There just happened to be five ministers there. Luke's mentioning them shows that there was a recognition of their ministries. They recognized this team. It is important that we recognize the ministry in our local assembly--not just of administrative members, but the full complement of the fivefold ministry.

The fivefold ministry

In Paul's informative letter to the Corinthians, he wrote in the twelfth chapter:

> And God hath set some in the church, first apostles, secondarily prophets, thirdly teachers...(I Corinthians 12:28)

This is echoed clearly in the book of Ephesians:

> There is one body...but unto every one of us is given grace according to the measure of the gift of Christ...And He gave some apostles; and some, prophets; and some, evangelists; and some, pastors and teachers; for the perfecting of the saints, for the work of the ministry...(Ephesians 4:4,7,11-12) See Table 2, page 43.

The Apostle Paul instructed the churches to realize the fact that there is plurality of ministry: several ministers on a peer level in the local church.

NEW TESTAMENT DEFINITION

TABLE 2

THE WORK OF THE MINISTRY
(Ephesians 4:11-12)

(1) *A fivefold leadership*

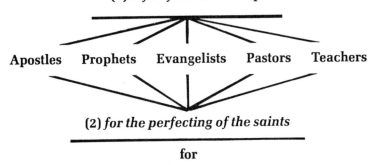

Apostles   Prophets   Evangelists   Pastors   Teachers

(2) *for the perfecting of the saints*

for

"the work of the ministry"

"for the edifying of the body of Christ"

It is God's desire that a team of spiritual elders "labor among and rule over" (I Thessalonians 5:12-13) the local congregation of saints. And it is His will that a variety of elders with differing gifts and roles comprise that team, so that the varying needs of the local gathering (Ephesians 4:11-12) can be met.

Christ warned his twelve disciples concerning the topic of governing the people:

But be not ye called Rabbi: for one is your Master even Christ; and all ye are brethren. And call no man your father upon the earth: for one is your Father, which is in heaven. Neither be called masters: for one is your Master, even Christ.

But he that is greatest among you shall be your servant. (Matthew 23:8-11)

TEAM MINISTRY

He emphasized the point that there is to be a peer relationship, with no one person dominating the spiritual rulership. There are to be no ranks, and no hierarchy: "You are all brethren." Of course, there are differing abilities, and different responsibilities contingent upon those abilities, among elders; but they all work side by side on a peer level.

The role of the senior elder

The question then arises: what about the need for a senior elder, or senior pastor, as he is usually called? Is he really necessary? The answer is yes. He is necessary. He is a vital part of the team. Because there is to be no domination, does not mean there is to be no leadership. The idea of plurality of elders does not take away the need for a recognition of a senior elder.

Wisdom tells us that every discussion group needs a leader or moderator. Every corporation board needs a chairperson. And every home needs a father figure who is the head. So every team of ministers needs a presiding elder, a senior elder. He is a "first among equals" and he merely keeps everything functioning smoothly and steadily.

Pre-eminence. This does not mean that, that individual dominates the group, or the team, or the home. John wrote concerning such a one who loved the high position:

> *I wrote unto the church; but Diotrephes, who loveth to have the pre-eminence among them, receiveth us not. (III John 9)*

> *...but do not ye after their works...but all their works they do for to be seen of men: they make broad their phylacteries, and enlarge the borders of their garments, and love the uppermost rooms at feasts, and the chief seats in the synagogues, and greetings in the markets...(Matthew 23:3,5-7)*

NEW TESTAMENT DEFINITION

The senior elder is not a coach who bosses all the players around, giving orders, and making all the decisions from the bench. If anything, he is a player-coach in the game, being an example to the other elders, and to the body. This service aspect is emphasized by Christ, who, while pre-eminent among the group of apostles being Chief Apostle (Hebrews 3:1; see also I Peter 2:25, Bishop), nevertheless served the other apostles (Luke 22:27; Matthew 20:28). Note also that Jesus warned:

> *...Ye know that they which are accounted to rule over the Gentiles exercise lordship over them; and their great ones exercise authority upon them. But so shall it not be among you: but whosoever will be great among you, shall be your minister: and whosoever of you will be the chiefest, shall be servant of all. (Mark 10:42-44)*

The senior elder serves the other team ministers by moderating, coordinating, encouraging, expediting, evaluating, alerting, motivating, and so forth, as well as moving in his specific spiritual gift to edify the body, as a whole. This role is vital to the smooth functioning of team ministry. It is of great importance as a role, but not as a rank.

An unfortunate example

There was a brother that went out from a local church, a young man with great promise. He was one of those budding preachers that had to argue everything through.

After a few months of pioneering a new church, it was rumored that he did not agree with the basic concept of ministry and government that we are writing about here. He leaned toward the belief that he did not need the role of senior elder, or senior pastor.

"I believe everybody should be equal. We have three elders here, and we are all equal. We have to have a unanimous decision. And whoever wants to take charge

TEAM MINISTRY

on Sunday takes charge. We are just kind of led by the Spirit."

It was explained to him that there was a need for a senior elder to maintain a smooth running ministering team. But neither reason nor Scripture could reach him. The gentleman has a lovely family with children of an excellent spirit. His house is impeccable as far as order and discipline and love. His children are sweet, loving, outgoing, polite and courteous.

His church experienced very little growth for the next couple of years under his system of government and ministry.

A dream in the night

One night he had a dream, he and his family were going to a church service where a Christian movie was going to be shown. They arrived late for some reason and the movie had already started. He let his wife and children out of the car to go in and find seats while he parked. When he had parked the car, he entered the church building which had a balcony. It was dark inside since the movie had already begun. The usher mentioned that the only seats left were in the balcony. So he went to look for his family there. He didn't find them up there so he assumed they had found seats elsewhere.

He decided to sit in the balcony, since it was too dark to continue searching for them. Shortly after being seated, somebody began yelling, FIRE! FIRE! FIRE! Pandemonium erupted. His dream turned into a nightmare. Everyone was running in all directions.

Jumping up he rushed around, struggling through the crowd, fearing for the safety of his family.

Then suddenly he found his wife. But the children were nowhere to be seen.

"Where are the children?" he cried out to her. "I

thought the children were with you!"

When his wife saw that he was alone, she too, began to panic, "I thought they were with you!"

He responded in disbelief, "But I thought you had them!"

"No, I thought you had them," she echoed.

Then suddenly he woke up from his dream.

Almost instantly, as he hastily reviewed the dream, the Lord impressed upon him: "Somebody has got to be responsible! Somebody has got to be responsible!"

God knows what he is doing when he places ministries in the church with their respective roles. There is an extreme on the one hand, where the pastor is dictatorial and untouchable. But, on the other hand, there is an extreme of doing away with the role of the senior elder altogether, which means nobody is responsible.

Look at the synagogues

There seems to be universal agreement among theological scholars that the authority of the synagogue in every normal case is in the hands of a small body of elders. One of the later Psalms mentions "the congregation of the people and the assembly of the elders" (Psalm 107:32).

The smallest recognized quorum was three elders. If three suitable elders were not available, a single teacher could preside in a synagogue. But he could make no authoritative decision, either doctrinal or practical. He had to have other elders associated with him.

President of the eldership

Each council of elders had a president, or chairman who was appointed for life. He could be removed for a time, or permanently, because of sin. The term found often in the New Testament "ruler of the synagogue" may refer to

TEAM MINISTRY

this person. It could also refer to other prominent and honored elders in the council as well (Luke 8:41,49).

The president of the elders was always of the same order and office with the rest of the council, although it is granted that he usually was distinguished beyond the other elders in lieu of his ability and dignity. But he was always subject to the council, his peers, who could remove him from his office. And he could do nothing without them.

Example of the Jewish church

The earliest Christians undoubtedly felt quite natural in patterning the early local gatherings of believers along the lines of the synagogue system of government: plurality of elders with a senior or presiding elder. James, the brother of Jesus, seems to have been the senior elder in Jerusalem (Acts 15:13). Titus was a prominent facilitator in Crete (Titus 1:5). And John was probably a senior elder in an Asian church (II John 1). But each acted in conjunction with the elder council. When the final draft of the letter commending the new Gentile converts was written, it came from "the apostles and elders and brethren" in general, as a unified body (Acts 15:23).

All of these examples document that team ministry is not a new scheme for the traditional pastor to use to unload some of his burdensome responsibilities. It is not a new fad. Rather, it is a well-proven form of government and ministry which the apostles implemented effectively in establishing God's Kingdom through the local church. And God blessed this design for accomplishing His purposes of ministry to the body and to the world by His Holy Spirit. The early church prospered and spread rapidly, and eventually turned the whole Roman world upside down (Acts 17:6).

NEW TESTAMENT DEFINITION

One pastor cannot be involved in the many areas traditionally dropped into his lap. It was not God's intention that he be a one-man show or, a jack-of-all-trades. The "my-boat" attitude is too inadequate with such a large sea of people who are crying for help. It is going to take a boat with many hands manning the oars to accomplish the saving of lives and souls. This is why we say that team ministry is crucial to effective church life.

PART FIVE

The awesome benefits of developing team ministry

We have seen how the Old Testament first laid out patterns of team ministry. And we have reviewed the New Testament definition of ministry. Now we are going to look at the tremendous benefits derived from following this Biblical pattern. As Psalm 103:5 suggests: the fruit is sweet to taste and health to the bones.

I. A TOTAL MINISTRY

The first benefit that becomes evident is total ministry. When you have men with different ministries and roles working together, you have a complete ministry. A complete ministry is the only kind of ministry that can properly take care of all the needs of the sheep.

Ministers, in the natural realm, do not all have the same abilities or talents. Where one excels, another is deficient. Where one is amateur, another is professional. Where one has insight, another is unenlightened. Where one is called, another is forbidden. Where one flows, another is struggling. But when you put all these together in a team, you have an awesome potential for success.

There are different grace-gifts

In the spiritual and supernatural realm, God bestows differing and various gifts and calls upon individuals according to His will:

> But unto every one of us is given grace according to the measure of the gift of Christ. Wherefore He saith, When He ascended upon high, He led captivity captive, and gave gifts unto men...and He gave some apostles; and some, prophets; and some, evangelists; and some, pastors and teachers. (Ephesians 4:7-8,11)

AWESOME BENEFITS

And, the exciting passage in the Bible:

> *Now there are diversities of gifts, but the same Spirit. And there are differences of administrations, but the same Lord. And there are diversities of operations, but it is the same God which worketh all in all. But the manifestation of the Spirit is given to every man to profit withal.*
>
> *For to one is given by the Spirit the word of wisdom; to another the word of knowledge by the same Spirit; to another faith by the same Spirit; to another the gifts of healing by the same Spirit; to another the working of miracles; to another prophecy; to another discerning of spirits; to another divers kinds of tongues; to another the interpretation of tongues.*
>
> *But all these worketh that one and the selfsame Spirit, dividing to every man severally as He will. For as the body is one, and hath many members, and all the members of that one body, being many, are one body: so also is Christ. (I Corinthians 12:4-12)*
>
> *And God hath set some in the church, first apostles, secondarily prophets, thirdly teachers, after that miracles, then gifts of healing, helps, governments, diversities of tongues.*
>
> *Are all apostles? are all prophets? are all teachers? are all workers of miracles?*
>
> *Have all the gifts of healing? do all speak with tongues? do all interpret? (I Corinthians 12:28-30)*

Here Paul states that there are different ministries, but they all can work together as a team because they have the same Spirit, the same Lord, and the same God.

Remember the parental team

Go back to the natural again to illustrate a spiritual truth. In a husband and wife, we have a team ministry on a peer level but with role differences. We are not in competition with each other. As a husband, I recognize my wife's role; and she, in turn, recognizes my role. I do not look at her as inferior, but rather as an equal. I do not think of her as not being as smart as me. Once in awhile we will have

TEAM MINISTRY

a tongue-in-cheek argument as to who really is the smartest! But to be really honest, I look at her wisdom as absolutely essential to my ministry, as well as my marriage. And I listen to her.

Still a young man when I was first married, my chauvinistic spirit would not allow that. If she said something, I tended to claim just the opposite--and get into trouble. I learned the hard way that when she would speak that was the other part of "me" talking. So I started listening to her. (At first I didn't let her know I was listening; I would just respond to what she said.)

I found out she had a sensitivity that I didn't have. She would come to me and say something like: "Brother and Sister _____ are having trouble."

"What do you mean, they're having trouble?" I would ask.

"Well, they're just not doing well, something's wrong."

"What do you mean? They're coming to church, aren't they? They're in prayer meeting, aren't they?"

"Well, you can just tell they're having trouble. Watch them. You'll see."

"But I am watching them. I am their watchman. Are you sure it's just not suspicion? You don't have any facts, do you? I've got enough other things to worry about."

Well. Guess what? Before very long I would hear a knock on my door. In would come Brother_____.

"I've got to talk to you, pastor, My wife just left me!"

My wife's words echoed in my ears: "They're having trouble, dear. Something's wrong."

That's one of the ways I discovered the value of team ministry. Nobody has it all. Even if you are the pastor, you have got to recognize that you don't have it all. And that is no threat to your role! If you're wise you will understand that the ministry is not to be dependent on one man. You will begin to recognize that God sovereignly brings team members together, just like in marriage.

He sovereignly does it. He brings them into the church. Even I had to awaken to this fact: I'm not supposed to have all the answers. It is not a threat to me or my ministry to need someone else.

No one minister is going to be an apostle, prophet, evangelist, pastor and teacher all rolled up into one. Different men have different expertise. Just as a wife has one type of expertise and a husband has another. So also the different ministries in leadership each demonstrate special expertise. Put them altogether and you have a total ministry.

Two ministries in one

Many times two ministries like apostle and prophet are mentioned together in the Bible:

> *...built upon the foundation of the apostles and prophets..." (Ephesians 2:20; see also Revelation 18:20)*

Let us analyze this a little bit. Prophets tend to be visionary. They tend to be up in the "heavenlies." But apostles, in establishing local churches, tend to be more practical in their approach to given situations.

If the church followed the prophets all the time, they might get off into all sorts of strange and extreme things. They might know the mind of God in what direction to go, but they wouldn't know how to carry it out in the most practical way. The result could be a tangled up mess in no time!

On the other hand, consider the apostle who complements the prophet's ministry. The apostle needs the visionary direction and inspiration of the prophet. Otherwise, the apostle's ministry would become bogged down in practical drudgery. The church needs the understanding in the spiritual realm that the prophet has. But the prophet would have a hard time being the pastor

TEAM MINISTRY

if he were to try to go it alone.

In my case, I admit to being pragmatic by nature. That's the kind of person I am. If it doesn't work, I am not interested. If it doesn't produce fruit, I just can't get enthused. If someone approaches me with a new idea and one or two Scriptures to back it up, I'll respond by asking, "Does it work in real life?" Any project or program in the local church has to work or I'm not interested.

In earlier years, I did not always have a great appreciation for prophets. Later, I began to realize that their role is essential in the house of God. Today, I listen to the prophetic word when it is given. In my church, I now have several powerful men who minister with the gift of prophecy. And I listen to them. When one responds to this kind of ministry in this manner it is amazing how that ministry complements all of the others in the body. And that's what happens with all of the fivefold ministries. They complement each other in the work of the Lord.

As every man hath received the gift, even so minister the same one to another, as good stewards of the manifold grace of God. (I Peter 4:10)

When the team complements each other, ministers to each other, and builds up each other, it is demonstrating to the body at large how "body ministry" works. What's more, the team ministers become examples to the congregation as to how they are to function in relation to each other. This is how the total ministry benefits the whole body.

II. A VARIETY OF MINISTRIES

The second benefit of team ministry is the variety of ministries that it brings to the sheep in the church. The ministers on a team have different personalities as the sheep to whom they minister are different, also. Individual sheep relate to some ministries more readily than they do to others. Where there are a variety of ministers to whom the sheep relate, they flourish best under team ministry.

The case of Barnabas and John Mark

The book of Acts relates the incident of Paul's rejection of John Mark as a traveling companion. He considered John to be a weak-kneed, spineless creature under pressure. He just could not relate to John Mark:

> *But Paul thought not good to take him with them, who departed from them from Pamphylia, and went not with them to the work. And the contention was so sharp between them, that they departed asunder one from the other: and so Barnabas took Mark...(Acts 15:38-39)*

Whether it was a ministry clash, a personality clash, or whatever, they just could not relate. Paul, with his dynamic personality, perhaps his nervous energy, could not flow with John Mark. Nor could he minister to the needs of John Mark.

Paul's teammate, however, could and did minister to John Mark. Barnabas saw the potential in the future of John Mark, and he had the patience to minister to John's need. Later on in Paul's ministry, after John was developed in the skills of ministry and had his young quirks ironed out, Paul saw that John was "profitable." Barnabas had accomplished in John Mark's life what Paul could not do.

The exciting variety which is available in team ministry frequently proves to be a lifesaver for the sheep. Take some sheep, for example, who cannot relate to the senior pastor. They are able to relate intimately with one of the other elders: a prophet, an evangelist, or a teacher. The result: that lamb doesn't have to leave the church in search of another fold to find food or green pasture. There is someone else on the team to minister to his needs. What's more, in due time he may find an affinity

TEAM MINISTRY

with the senior pastor through the developing ministry of one of the other elders.

Teamwork in Acts

Luke records in Acts the names of a ministering team in the city of Antioch:

> Now there were in the church that was at Antioch certain prophets and teachers; as Barnabas, and Simeon that was called Niger, and Lucius of Cyrene, and Manaen, which had been brought up with Herod the tetrarch, and Saul. As they ministered to the Lord...(Acts 13:1,2)

Barnabas was a soft-mannered Jew. There was a man named Simeon, also known as Niger (which means black). Lucius was probably a Greek, since it is a Greek name; he was a Gentile from Africa. Then we have Manaen, perhaps well educated having been brought up with the aristocrat, Herod (was half Jew and half Idumean). Then there was Saul, a religiously educated man from Asia Minor.

What a mixture! There was no racial boundaries. I like that. They were men of different backgrounds, training, and race. A theologian. An aristocrat. A prophet. A teacher. And one with a pastor's heart. But what a powerful team!

A lot of pastors do not like it when everyone does not fit into the same mold. Some denominations thrive on everyone doing the same thing, in the same way, with the same tone of voice, the same gestures.

I had to adjust my thinking, too. I had to change to fit the Biblical pattern. I had to recognize and appreciate variety in other ministries. But that is what makes a team. I know of two elders in a large church in another country. They merged two churches together a number of years ago. But the unique thing was that these two ministers are complete opposites in personality.

One minister is a very strong and powerful man. He is a big, robust, cowboy type: "Let's go get 'em. Round 'em up." And I mean that respectfully.

The other minister has a lot more finesse. He carries himself with the dignity of a high office. He is just the opposite in speech and mannerisms. To see these two ministers come together, merge as one team, and complement each other was awesome. Together they saw their church grow, and a Bible college became established. Their ministries provided variety for the people.

In the church I have served for nearly thirty years at this writing, we have elders on the team who are reserved and quiet (excellent counselors, and men of deep wisdom). Some of the sheep are really fed by them. We have other ministers who are analytical, probing, and excellent in making outlines (superb teachers). Some of the sheep love to sit at their feet. And then we have robust, inspiring trumpeters (dynamic prophets). Many sheep relate to them. And then there are sensitive, discerning elders (men with a shepherd's heart). Many sheep are watered by them until their thirst is quenched.

Not all sheep relate to the prophets. Or, to some other ministry. But they are blessed by at least one of the elders. In this way, the church as a whole is edified. The result is the church, with its variety of team ministers, provides a variety of options for the sheep, and the sheep grow in maturity and number.

Now he that planteth and he that watereth are one...for we are labourers together with God...(I Corinthians 3:8-9)

III. AN ACCELERATING PRODUCTIVITY

The third area of benefit from team ministry is the way in which it accelerates productivity. More work can come to fruition by the labors of several people, coordinated and working together, than by the same number of people

TEAM MINISTRY

working alone, or separately. Listen to Solomon, the wise King:

Two are better than one; because they have a good reward for their labour...if one prevail against him, two shall withstand him; and a threefold cord is not quickly broken. (Ecclesiastes 4:9,12)

In the physical, one strong man may be able to lift two hundred pounds, when he tries to lift the object alone. Two strong men may be able to lift four hundred pounds if they work separately at the job. But two men working together are able to lift the four hundred pounds plus several more pounds as well.

In another example, three cords of twine may be able to sustain a weight of say twenty pounds each when suspended separately. But when bound together the threefold cord will easily hold up the sixty pounds and then go on to sustain another hundred or so pounds on top of that!

The reward of men working together is not merely doubled when two join hands, or tripled when three work together; instead the reward increases in geometric proportions. Moses brought out this same principle five hundred years earlier:

How should one chase a thousand, and two put ten thousand to flight...(Deuteronomy 32:30)
(The answer: with the help of the Lord)

It might be that Jesus Christ had the threefold cord in mind when He instructed His disciples:

Again I say unto you, That if two of you shall agree on earth as touching any thing that they shall ask, it shall be done for them of My Father which is in heaven. For where two or three are gathered together in My name, there am I in the midst of them. (Matthew 18:19-20)

60

AWESOME BENEFITS

As in the physical illustrations, the same applies to the spiritual realm. More victories over spiritual evil can be accomplished when several men of God are agreeing, coordinating and focusing their efforts on the same issue.

An example of this is Paul's preaching at Athens. There was little fruit there, few converts to Christianity. But Paul was preaching alone. He had gone there alone. When Paul left there and went to Corinth, he met other brethren, Silas and Timothy, and became bold (Acts 18:1-11). A large church was established there as a result. Men ministering as a team achieve more than one working alone, and also, more than several working separately.

The principle: team ministry accelerates productivity.

IV. REITERATION OF TRUTH

Another benefit of team ministry is that it enhances another Biblical principle: truth reiterated establishes truth. That principle was first recorded by Moses and then re-emphasized in the New Testament:

> ...at the mouth of two witnesses, or at the mouth of three witnesses, shall the matter be established. (Deuteronomy 19:15)

> ...take with thee one or two more, that in the mouth of two or three witnesses every word may be established. (Matthew 18:16)

> This is the third time I am coming to you. In the mouth of two or three witnesses shall every word be established. (II Corinthians 13:1)

We realize that the subject here is primarily that of discipline and witnessing in a trial, where an event or statement by a party must be shown to be true beyond any doubt, or beyond a reasonable doubt. When two or three different individuals speak forth the same truth, it tends to establish that truth.

In the same way, a team of voices speaking the same thing can be very effective in establishing the truths of God in the hearts and lives of people.

TEAM MINISTRY

It is reassuring to the ears of the congregation when different ministers confirm the same thing from different viewpoints. One minister may preach on a truth needed for a specific time in the life of the church. Another may prophesy the same message. A third may dig into the Hebrew and Greek and show the basis for the same truth. And when they have all spoken, one cannot escape the conclusion, God is trying to tell us something, and we had better pay attention to it.

Thus truth emanating from two or three sources tends to establish truth.

V. ENCOURAGES NEW IDEAS

Another area of benefit is the infusion of new ideas. Because there are differences of ministries, there are differences of opinion. In team ministry one rubs shoulders with men who have different viewpoints, approaches and methods. The result can be enlightening. Problems you have been pondering for years can often be solved by listening to the different ideas of fellow-elders.

For some forty years I have been talking about certain things with my wife. At the same time, she has been talking to me about certain things. Each of us has been changing a little in the process. We just get in there and adjust each other. We are not afraid to disagree with each other. In the process we each gain new insight.

Truth can bear inspection. If someone challenges what you believe you should not get upset. If what you believe is true, it will bear inspection. If it is error, it will fade away in the light of the truth. And if it fades away, your brother has done you a favor. But as one minister once said: "A man who lives alone thinks his own thoughts." He never has the benefit of cross-examination to seek out error and to reinforce truth.

The elders where I minister have outstanding talks and confabs. We discuss many problems on a peer level. If you sat in on some of our eldership meetings you might wonder if we really get along together because everyone is free to voice his opinion. Bang! Bang! Bang! We go back and forth over issues and search out all of the options.

On some issues we may take two years to come to a consensus. But it's amazing. It is possible to give free expression to your opinion and never break rank, never break the unity of the spirit, never break fellowship. We have all these opinions and views, but suddenly it all comes together. God brings unity in decisions: decisions which were based on openmindedness and a free flow of ideas. That is one of the beautiful benefits of team ministry.

> *Behold, how good and how pleasant it is for brethren to dwell together in unity! It is like the precious ointment upon the head, that ran down upon the beard, even Aaron's beard...(Psalm 133:1-2)*

VI. CHECKS AND BALANCES--A BONUS BENEFIT

This by-product of team ministry--checks and balances--is much needed in the church. Peter warned the elders in his letter:

> *Feed the flock of God which is among you, taking the oversight thereof, not by constraint, but willingly; not for filthy lucre, but of a ready mind; neither as being lords over God's heritage, but being ensamples to the flock. (I Peter 5:2-3)*

The very fact that he warned these elders not to abuse the eldership, either by covetousness, by begrudged necessity, or being power hungry, shows that it could be abused. That danger is ever present. It is a threat that lurks in the shadows of every parsonage.

A parental example

As parents, we could lord it over our children, couldn't we? We could beat them. We could be cruel to them.

TEAM MINISTRY

We could demand more from them than they could handle. We could line them up and discipline them until we broke their spirits (Ephesians 6:4; Colossians 3:21).

Your response might be "Yes, you could do that. But that's not the way to raise a family!" A family best functions when the parents lead their children and train them by example.

The same principle applies in the house of God. We have been given the responsibility of ruling, as well as teaching, and caring. And just as God never entrusted the family unit to one person because each person needs checks and balances, so also the church needs team ministry for checks and balances.

If I begin to get a little bit too harsh or too strong with my children--I have four beautiful daughters--guess who takes care of dad? My wife will say, "Honey, I'd like to talk to you in the back room." And we go back there, and I know I am in trouble!

"I don't think you're being fair to the children," she would begin.

"What do you mean I'm not fair?"

"You didn't listen to them. Now this is what they really said. This is what they asked when you said, 'No'."

"Oh, is that what they said? Oh, well I don't mind them doing that!"

Maybe you don't have the kind of discussion in your home, but we do. And it illustrates the kinds of checks and balances that pastors can have in a team ministry.

The temptations and pitfalls of a minister may be summed up in four categories: (1) those that involve the MIND (exaltation of self); (2) those that involve MONEY (embezzlement of gold or silver); (3) those that involve MORALITY (entanglement with sex); and (4) those that involve MISGIVINGS (embitterment in sorrow). The first three are renowned and easily discerned when the tragedy has happened. The fourth one isn't talked about much but it is just as deadly in destroying a man and the ministry God has given him.

Love not the world, neither the things that are in the world. If any man love the world, the love of the Father is not in him. For all that is in the world, the lust of the flesh, and the lust of the eyes, and the pride of life, is not of the Father...(I John 2:15-16)

Looking diligently lest any man fail of the grace of God; lest any root of bitterness springing up trouble you, and thereby many be defiled; lest there be any fornicator, or profane person, as Esau, who for one morsel of meat sold his birthright. (Hebrews 12:15-16)

When a man tries to minister alone he expands his vulnerability, and enlarges the number of opportunities for temptation. Every man has his blind spots, character flaws that he cannot see, or wishes not to see. The objective eyes of a brother or counsellor are often needed to make one aware of these danger areas. But if he ministers alone he invites disaster with open arms.

Ambition. Besides character flaws in a minister's human nature, the very nature of the minister's role adds more temptation: prominence, authority, and ruling. Many a great man has fallen through blind ambition. The Babylonian king was not the first, and certainly not the last to be blinded:

For thou hast said in thine heart, I will ascend into heaven, I will exalt my throne above the stars of God: I will sit upon the mount of the congregation, in the sides of the north: I will ascend above the heights of the clouds; I will be like the most High. Yet thou shalt be brought down to hell, to the sides of the pit. (Isaiah 14:13-15)

And in the New Testament, Herod seems to have been blinded to this Old Testament example of certain just reward:

And upon a set day Herod, arrayed in royal apparel, sat upon his throne, and made an oration unto them. And the people gave a shout,

TEAM MINISTRY

*saying, It is the voice of a god, and not of a man. And immediately
the angel of the Lord smote him, because he gave not God the glory:
and he was eaten of worms, and gave up the ghost. (Acts 12:21-23)*

That comet-like feeling of being able to dazzle people
with elocution is as momentary as a comet in the galaxy
which appears briefly then vanishes into the vast darkness.
Yet without other team ministers to bring one down to
earth after delivering great sermons, a person can easily
rise to the place of "thinking more highly of himself than
he ought" (Romans 12:3; Galatians 6:3; I Corinthians 8:2).
What a value other ministers on our team can be when
they balance our fantasies with reality, when they check
our unchecked opinions of ourselves.

*Two are better than one...for if they fall, the one will lift up his fellow:
but woe to him that is alone when he falleth; for he hath not another
to help him up. (Ecclesiastes 4:9-10)*

Money Matters. If I were to ask any young fledgling
entering the ministry if he intended to dip into the
collection plate, embezzle, or misappropriate church funds,
he would most certainly be offended and resound with a
hearty, No! However, when handling finances alone,
opportunities lend themselves without any invitation, and
without any warning. It can start by simple mistakes in
counting the offering, or honestly forgotten funds, or a
misplaced tithe envelope found later (which no one ever
missed). But that seed of temptation is like dandelion or
morning glory weeds: once it gets started it is hard to root
out.

When a minister falls financially, Satan has a way of
making sure that the whole city finds out about it. The
news media jumps on the story, and the whole ministry is
branded as greedy money-grabbers.

I can remember in my own ministry, when I was
extremely thankful that we had an alert financial manager

in the church to check and follow up on any irregularity. I had been invited to speak at a ministers' convention. It was the custom for our church to purchase the plane tickets with the understanding that the money would be reimbursed by those who had invited me to speak. In the weeks that followed they sent the money to my home, and through an honest mistake (the excitement of the meeting, my busy schedule, the busy affairs of home life) it was inadvertently placed in my personal bank account.

It was not long until I heard a knock on my door. When I opened it there stood our church treasurer. The next few moments were the most embarrassing I have ever experienced, even though it was an honest mistake. After he left, I sat down and thought about it. This thought of knowing that there were others checking to keep the ministry pure made me appreciate team ministry even more. What a precious built-in safeguard team ministry really is.

Discernment. Some men are able to hide their problems better than others. Or, at least, they are able to conceal their need until after it has blown up into a grand scale mess. But one of the grace gifts to the church is the gift of discernment (I Corinthians 12:10). And it is reassuring to know that there are elders on the team who will exercise this gift, that there are spiritual ministers who can zero in on a need before disaster strikes. God has given a supernatural dimension of checks and balances to the church when they function according to this plan of team ministry.

VII. ASSURES SMOOTH TRANSITION

Another peaceful, relaxing benefit of team ministry is the facilitation of a smooth transition from one pastor or elder to another. Having a pastor leave a church can be a very traumatic experience for any congregation to handle.

TEAM MINISTRY

Uncertainty and anxiety often dominate the mood of the congregation.

Sometimes a committee is selected to do painstaking research, interviewing, scrutinizing and selecting, hoping that they make a right choice. Then there is a trial period with mutual anxiety on the part of the newly selected minister, as well as the people. Sometimes there is an occasion for choosing sides, division, bitterness, rejection, and party-spirit. Often it takes years for emotional and spiritual healing to mend the rifts and hurts.

It is most certain that in the life of a local church a minister is going to leave the scene. This may be either because of death, illness, retirement, or simply new direction in a minister's life. Sometimes the change is unexpected and sudden. Other times it is ordered and planned. But change is certain.

Just as in a family setting, the children need to feel warmth and security. A divorce upsets that much needed security. So also in a local church environment, the sheep need security. Sheep like the serenity of green pastures and still waters (Psalm 23). They need calm and orderly transition from one shepherd to another.

Team ministry provides this serene transition. When one member leaves, the rest of the elders are able to continue feeding the flock. When a new elder emerges from the congregation to take the senior elder's place, there is a smooth and calm atmosphere. The people sense this security and appreciate it.

Luke gave us an example of this smooth transition when the elders at Antioch sent out Paul and Barnabas to do apostolic work (Acts 13:2). The other elders continued to maintain the flow of ministry to the congregation of believers.

The Lord is concerned about his flock. He does not wish them to be hurt or scattered, to use the descriptive words of the prophet:

...smite the shepherd, and the sheep shall be scattered: and I will turn my hand upon the little ones. (Zechariah 13:7; compare Matthew 26:31 and Mark 14:27)

Even the chosen apostles fled in confusion, and hid in fear and secrecy, when their shepherd was taken from them. Team ministry is a blessing to the flock.

VIII. PROVIDES FULFILLMENT

Still another blessing in team ministry is the opportunity of ministers to find satisfying and complete fulfillment in life. In the past, when a young man felt the call of the Lord to public ministry, he was sent to some remote pioneer work. He went there, struggled at pastoring for months and sometimes years, not doing very well. He may spend his whole life with thirty people at the most. As new ones came in, old members left. He seemed never to make any progress. He never found fulfillment in his calling. Yet he knows that God had called him to be a minister.

The problem lies in the fact that while he did have ministerial ability and a calling, it was not to a pastoral role. There are five different ministerial roles mentioned by Paul (Ephesians 4:11). In the pioneer setting, he was required to do all five. What a frustration. What an exercise in mediocrity. By being required to try vainly to fulfill all roles, he became a jack-of-all-trades, and a master of none. And the result: no satisfying fulfillment.

Measure of Grace. To each minister is given different grace-gifts, different measures of grace:

But unto every one of us is given according to the measure of the gift of Christ. (Ephesians 4:7)

For I say...to every man that is among you, not to think of himself more highly than he ought to think; but to think soberly, according as God hath dealt to every man the measure of faith. For as we have

TEAM MINISTRY

many members in one body, and all members have not the same office: so we, being many, are one body in Christ, and every one members one of another. Having them gifts differing according to the grace that is given to us...(Romans 12:3-6)

The Romans seem to have had the same problem many ministers have today. They think they can do it all. Self-sufficiency was their curse, their secret sin. As a result they were, albeit unwittingly, thinking more highly of themselves than they ought to have been thinking.

The admonition of Paul is to think soberly, that is, to realize your limitations. Sober thinking says, "I need other team elders." Sober thinking cries out, "If I am going to find satisfying fulfillment in my ministry, I must stick to my ministry, and not try to do someone elses." Sober thinking proclaims, "Team ministry will keep me from majoring in mediocrity."

For an example, I think of an evangelist that I know. He is an evangelist if I've ever seen an evangelist. That man just eats it up! It was one of the greatest things that happened to the church he attended when the elders recognized where he really fit. He's not what you would call a theologian, but he has contributed to his church by stirring it to active aggressive outreach. He has inspired dozens of believers to go door-to-door, and to hit the streets witnessing and evangelizing.

We have always thought of an evangelist as someone who wore white shoes, a brightly colored jacket, played a guitar, and gave stirring altar calls. Or, we have conceived of him as a city-wide organizer who blitzes the media, then rents the civic auditorium, and holds a crusade. But if we forced the elder with an evangelistic ministry into that mold, he most likely would never make it. He could not survive as a preaching evangelist. Nor is he a one-man show. However, brought on to a team where his weaknesses can be covered by other brethren, he becomes a strong minister.

Another minister I am thinking of was trained in college and in seminary. However, he just did not have the one-man pastoral ability. But when you put him on a team, he was powerful. Alone he would be frustrated and unfruitful even though he was called of God as any other minister. On a team he becomes a powerful man of God. And he contributed to several churches in a mighty way.

The church must rid itself of the mentality that to be a minister one must be able to be a solo minister. We have depleted the church of strength because we have sent men off to go it alone, instead of making them part of a team where they can major in their own unique gift. Our whole concept of ministry has to be readjusted. When that happens, all of a sudden we will see all these men around us, right in our midst, who have strength, and who have much to offer in their area of expertise, in their God-given role.

Some men are excellent teachers. But they are not gatherers. People are not attracted to them personally. They do not have gathering ability. But how are they going to teach unless some other minister has the ability to gather them? With a team, the ministers are released to excel in their specific areas. This release brings a sense of satisfaction and a joy of fulfillment in life. Without a team there are going to be a lot of frustrated ministers preaching to a lot of frustrated congregations (with a lot of frustrated ministers' families feeling the brunt of it).

We can only release other ministers when we can relax in the fact that they are not competitors. They are not taking away from our ministry. Rather, they are enhancing it.

I cannot minister by myself. If I were all alone, I would fizzle out. I might be able to preach. But I need teachers around me. I need also that prophetic mantle around me. I tell the prophets in our church, "When you get moving in your ministry, you release me to go forward

TEAM MINISTRY

in my ministry."

Sometimes a minister walks onto the platform as if it were a dry desert. His emotions are just as dead and barren. He stands there knowing that trying to preach is going to be like spitting cotton. But then someone stands up and with a prophetic mantle upon him begins to prophesy the Word of the Lord. All of a sudden your heart will just come alive because the Word confirms the message about to be delivered. Now the Lord has spoken, who can help but minister:

> *Surely the Lord God will do nothing, but He revealeth His secret unto His servants the prophets. The lion hath roared, who will not fear? the Lord God hath spoken, who can but prophesy? (Amos 3:7-8)*

After the prophets have spoken, I just can't wait to get into the pulpit.

The church needs to recognize these various ministries and appreciate them. We need to help them surface, not think of them as a threat. I was told during my youth to watch out for ex-ministers or ex-preachers if they come into your church. They will split your church. This advice did not take into consideration that there was a lot of frustrated potential bound up in the hearts of these men.

We do have a number of ex-ministers in our body that are now elders. They are doing great. Out there they were pushed into a role that was not theirs. Yet they were called of God as much as any minister. When they finally started moving as part of a team, they came alive and began to prosper in their ministry. The exuberant sense of fulfillment beamed on their faces.

The joy of their ministry is now felt in the congregation of the righteous. The stigma of "You didn't quite make it alone," or "You couldn't handle a thirty member church" has faded into meaninglessness under the bright light of fulfillment in team ministry.

AWESOME BENEFITS

God simply doesn't design people--and ministers are people--to go it alone. Not in family life. Not in ministerial life. Nor in any other aspect of life.

IX. FACILITATES GROWTH

Team ministry is also profitable because it best facilitates growth. In fact, in most cases it provides a growth factor that has unlimited potential.

The pressures and stress that accompany continuing growth are too much for any one man to bear alone. It is just common sense that more people require more attention, and make more demands on a minister's time and resources.

A team can shoulder the "growing pains" with much more ease than a single pastor ever could.

Notice also that doubling the number of elders in a growing church does not merely double the number of people the elders can handle. Instead, the number of people the elders can manage increases geometrically in proportion. Just as one puts a thousand and two put ten thousand to flight (Deuteronomy 32:30) so also the additional minister increases the ability to minister life by more than just double. It increases the capability phenomenally.

X. AND IT PRESERVES MINISTERS

Perhaps the greatest blessing of team ministry is that it preserves ministers. Ministers are people too. We are subject to all of the frailties of every man, physically and emotionally.

As great a man as Elijah was, with the power to offer prayers that resulted in tremendous miracles, he was still "a man subject to like passions as we are" (James 5:17). As great as the apostles and prophets in the New Testament were, Paul and Barnabas, yet they admitted that they were men of "like passions with you" (Acts 14:15).

This frailty is subject to burnout. People in all phases of social work suffer from burnout: doctors, nurses, social workers, psychiatrists, and ministers. The stress of dealing with other people's problems (hang-ups, tragedies and sorrows, deaths, setbacks and losses) can be overwhelming.

Putting the load of the pastorate on one man can be devastating at best, life-destroying at the worst. (See Table 3, page 75.) But when the load of a growing church is shared by a team of elders (see Table 4, page 75), the benefits to the whole church and the pastor are indeed tremendous! As well as, lifesaving!

P.S. It's lonely at the top

It can be lonely if one has to listen to all the needs of the people and try to solve them alone. It can be fatal to the minister. He needs someone on his peer level to whom he can talk. Ministers also need someone in whom they can confide. It's hard to talk to someone who is not a minister, lest their confidentiality be betrayed. It's a touchy situation in which ministers find themselves.

Ministers need close companionship, just like other humans. Yet often the members of the congregation unwittingly shut them out from vital fellowship because the pastor is presumed to be a special breed of man, apart from the rest of humanity.

Early in 1984, the president of a major protestant denomination was addressing a gathering of over 10,000 people from various denominational backgrounds and theologies. Discussing the relationship of pastor and people in his presentation, he referred to the hunger in many a pastor's heart for one of his laymen to come up, and put his arms around him and say, "Pastor. We're with you. We love you."

On the platform with a group of ministers was a

AWESOME BENEFITS

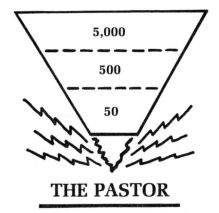

TABLE 3

The hurting church—one man rule. One pastor carrying the whole load.

THE PASTOR

TABLE 4

The healthy, growing church with a team of ministering elders... training the saints for the work of the ministry.

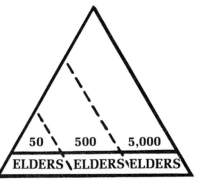

TEAM MINISTRY

prominent Christian author who stepped up to the speaker, threw his arms around him and said, "Forgive me brother. I have failed to pray for you as I should, I love you as my brother." A hush swept over the audience as for a few minutes the two men on the platform embraced and sobbed together.

Then wiping away his tears, this giant of a man returned to his message after saying, "Many is the time in my ministry that I would have given everything in the world to have one of the laymen in my church do that for me. What a load it might have taken off of my shoulders."

And then he proceeded to complete his address. But somehow in God's sovereignty the tone and response seemed to be different from that point on.

Most ministers have learned to paste on that professional smile by the time they have left seminary or Bible college. But underneath that smile is the face of a real man who needs encouragement. He needs exhortation. And he needs understanding. What greater source of understanding could there be than from another minister? What greater application for a man's effort and struggles could there be than that which arises from another minister who is so familiar with them himself?

Yes, the benefits of team ministry are awesome. After twenty-three years of ministry in one church, I believe they are essential to continued growth as well as being lifesaving to the senior minister.

PART SIX

Guidelines for setting up a team ministry in your church

In this section, I would like to share some guidelines for beginning a team ministry in a local church that is presently governed by another form of leadership. These are guidelines gleaned from the Bible, and buttressed by some thirty years experience as a senior minister in one church. They are not meant to be hard and fast rules as far as application in different cultures and communities. They lend themselves to flexibility and adaptability depending upon the various situations in which a local church may find itself.

I. RETHINKING THE PASTOR'S DUTIES

First, the pastor's role has to be re-examined. The pastor himself must take a second look at what he is doing in practice. And he must re-evaluate what God intended him to do in reality. He must ask himself, "Is this what God intended me to be doing when he called me into the ministry?" All of us want to do God's will, but periodically we must evaluate our state of affairs and see if we really are doing God's intended will.

A conscientious minister will study the Word to discover God's plan for the ministry. He will seek the Bible's definition of what a pastor is and does. He will seek for the true meaning of eldership. One must know what he is desiring to accomplish before he starts trying to fulfill his role. He must discover what kind of pattern for spiritual leadership will best provide for the feeding, training, maturing, and ruling of the "flock of God" (Hebrews 13:7; I Peter 5:2; James 5:14).

ORGANIZATIONAL GUIDELINES

Vision. Once a minister knows these things he can set goals. He can place before himself a vision to aim toward. With this vision, he will not be sidetracked, or deterred by obstacles that will mysteriously spring up all around him. Voices of criticism, monetary hurdles, temptation to slip back into tradition will not be able to stop his progress because the vision in front of him will burn brightly. This new vision will be like "a burning fire shut up in my bones" that will continually beg for expression (Jeremiah 20:9). There will be no rest until fulfillment is accomplished. The vision will cause him to build for it, pray for it, wait for it, work for it, and then, rejoice in it with a great sense of meaningfulness when it comes to pass.

Confidence. With this new vision will come a single-mindedness that will produce courage and confidence. "This is what God wants, we will work until it is accomplished!" Faith and belief in the knowledge of what God has revealed to you will strengthen you as you take on new roles and responsibilities. Confidence is contagious. This confidence will gain for you the admiration of the people (Ephesians 6:19-20).

In rethinking the pastor's role, you may discover some quirks and fancies of your old human nature lurking in the shadows of your heart. For example, in examining the concept of team ministry you may discover that your gift and ability in the ministry is not best fulfilled as the senior elder and you would have to consider the possibility of your not being "senior" any more, but one of the other team members. In this change you may be taunted by the idea that you are "stepping down" or that you are being "demoted."

However, this is certainly not the case. The ministry is not a pyramid system, or a sales ladder, or an executive scramble to be number one. Being on a team is not God's "second best." But it is God's greatest design for you.

TEAM MINISTRY

When you cease from the scramble to be number one and settle into a position on a team that better fits your gifts and calling, a sense of fulfillment and release is certain to come your way. The frustration of trying to administer, for example, when your gift is teaching or preaching, is now all gone. Instead of frustration you now have the excitement and joy of fulfillment. What a release!

Status. Position does not equal value. Position does not determine value. The role that God has laid out for you in His predetermined counsel and forethought is the best thing that could ever happen to you. What God has uniquely designed for you as far as role is concerned is what is going to bring you the greatest joy in this life. It is not a mark of inferiority to no longer be the senior elder, or senior pastor. In Christianity it is not more glorious to be "on the top of the pile."

Fellow laborers. One learned teacher has said that as the glory of man is the woman, and the glory of Christ is his bride the church, so the glory of the senior elder is the team (II Corinthians 8:23). The Apostle Paul continually bragged on those who accompanied him in the ministry. He called them:

Fellow laborers (Philippians 4:3; I Thessalonians 3:2)

Fellow helpers (II Corinthians 8:23; III John 8)

Fellow servants (Colossians 1:7; 4:7)

Fellow soldiers (Philippians 2:25)

Fellow workers (Colossians 4:11)

Yoke fellows (Philippians 4:3)

It is no exaggeration to say that Paul's success in the ministry was in large part due to the comfort, encouragement, and support he received from the members of the teams that ministered alongside him. If Paul could appreciate and honor team members, then we should certainly not depreciate ourselves if we are not "the senior" pastor or elder. Rather, we must develop the conviction that "God has placed me in the position that I am in for His purpose, and my good."

The wife-husband example

A wife can find great joy in making her husband successful. And she is worthy of praise and honor when she does so (Proverbs 31). There is an inherent joy in making others successful. An "assist" in baskestball brings just as much satisfaction and is worthy of just as much honor, as is the "slam dunk." The crew of a space craft are just as important as are the pilots. What a joy it is to make someone else successful. We have all heard of the phrase: "I made him what he is today." It reflects a sense of fulfillment and accomplishment that is rarely exceeded in life. No wonder Jesus said:

> For whosoever will save his life shall lose it: and whosoever will lose his life for My sake shall find it. (Matthew 16:25; also I Corinthians 10:24 and Philippians 2:4)

Share and share alike. In rethinking the pastor's duties one must face the idea of doing more sharing. The senior elder no longer should be the bottleneck of the flow of the ministry. More than just in theory, the ministry must be shared in practice. There must be sharing on the platform with different ones leading the worship, the singing, the praying; yes, and even preaching. There must be sharing in pastoral ceremonies: various ones administer baptisms, dedications, weddings, and communions. There must be sharing in counselling and spiritual guidance.

Delegating. This is going to involve delegating responsibilities and even authority. Rethinking the ministry might mean relinquishing your grip on all the strings of the church. And only hanging on to those for which you are especially suited. The initial feeling might be that of "losing control." But in reality you are gaining the strength of many men. Your strength (which has been dissipated by petty decisions, burdensome tasks, menial chores, and dozens of other involvements) will suddenly return to you. And you will have new drive and vigor to accomplish your heart's desires. Instead of being tied down and bogged down, you will be released, set free to fulfill your calling.

A past president is said to have remarked that the best executive is the one who has sense enough to pick good men to do what he wants done, and self-restraint enough to keep from meddling with them while they do it! While that is not Scripture, it reflects the benefits of team ministry. Rethinking the roles of spiritual leadership may take hours of soul-searching, prayer and Bible study.

II. PERSUADING THE POWER STRUCTURE

The second necessary step is convincing the present governing body of the value of team ministry and the necessity of implementing it. Needless to say, this may be no easy task. But on the other hand, perhaps, just perhaps, the Lord has been doing some work in their hearts and minds, as well as in yours.

Instead of taking the attitude of fear, and thinking that it's going to be like fighting city hall, be positive and full of faith. They are not city hall. They are your brothers in Christ. They are not your enemies. They are as eager to do the will of God as you are.

> ...My doctrine is not mine, but His that sent me. If any man will do His will, he shall know of the doctrine, whether it be of God, or whether I speak of myself. (John 7:16-17)

> And be not conformed to this world: but be ye transformed by the renewing of your mind, that ye may prove what is that good, and acceptable, and perfect, will of God. For as we have many members in one body, and all members have not the same office. (Romans 12:2,4)

ORGANIZATIONAL GUIDELINES

Those in power who are sincere and fervent in seeking after God and who want His will done in all things, will have a listening ear to the voice of God. Those who diligently search out the Word to see whether these things be so will conform to its teachings. The Holy Spirit in them will testify to the truthfulness of this, or any valid doctrine or practice.

Patience. In the courting and romancing relationship, before marriage can occur, the Lord has to speak to the woman as well as to the man. Sometimes this takes a longer time than the impatient gentleman desires. But he still must wait. So also in this major change in the life of a local church. Great patience must be exercised in love.

Roadblocks. There are several reasons why a deacon board, trustee board, senior pastor, or democratic congregation may throw up roadblocks to the beginning of a new or unfamiliar idea. First of all, it is in the very nature of human beings in the "establishment" to be conservative, resist change.

This is a built-in protective guard in management-establishment governing bodies. Don't jump at every supposedly new fad that comes along. It is certainly reasonable for restraint to be employed when something new "threatens" the status quo. No one would like to be taken in by radical thinking only to find out later they were wrong.

There must then be patient teaching of the governing body and patience with the power structure. The Scriptures suggest caution and persistence in searching out what the Word has to say about it.

TEAM MINISTRY

...the honour of kings is to search out a matter. *(Proverbs 25:2)*

These were more noble than those in Thessalonica, in that they received the Word with all readiness of mind, and searched the Scriptures daily, whether those things were so. *(Acts 17:11)*

There is an old saying that goes something like this: "Men convinced against their will are of the same opinion still." If there is to be productive and effective change, there must be a depth of clear, plain Scriptural teaching.

One does not change just for change's sake. One changes because the Bible says this is the way to go. And along with Bible truth, needs to be a willing spirit to accept change when such change is shown to be beneficial.

It is good for a power structure to be protective and conservative. But it is also noble for it to conform to the will and mind of the Lord when that has been revealed. Dealing with men's minds involves teaching. Dealing with men's wills involves prayer and intercession before God.

Lack of teaching, the stubborn spirit of tradition, disunity of spirit, overprotectiveness, lack of a clear vision may be some of the things that will impede progress toward the establishment of team ministry. But we have the promise that the Lord will build His church (Matthew 16:18).

III. EDUCATING THE PEOPLE

This third guideline for change is extremely vital. The people in the congregation must be slowly and thoroughly educated in the truth. People are as sheep and when something new and sudden is thrust upon them they can lose their sense of security and become "spooked."

Fear, uncertainty, insecurity, misinformation, rumors and gossip can cause the sheep to panic and scatter, and figuratively, trample one another. A slow, patient and thorough teaching process must be implemented.

ORGANIZATIONAL GUIDELINES

This should be carried out in small teaching groups and also when the congregation convenes in public meetings. If the teaching is presented openly and honestly, rumors can quickly be laid to rest. A good plan for teaching should include most of the following points:

1. The dire need for team ministry
2. The Biblical plan of the local church ministry
3. The desire to maintain a vision to see the plan become reality
4. The real possibility of implementing it
5. The necessity of unity and harmony during change
6. The excitement that follows fulfilling God's will in His people

Excitement. It is exciting to see God's people respond to His will and plan: to rise up and say we can do it; to see them tackle problems and hurdles in stride; to maintain morale and harmony; for none of them to break rank; and for the stronger sheep to support the weaker sheep when the going gets tough; and then to hear the people shout in unison, "We have finished it! It is done!"

So built we the wall; and all the wall was joined together unto the half thereof: for the people had a mind to work. (Nehemiah 4:6)

But the people must hear a clear sound. Change must be well organized, coordinated, and planned. Everything must be done "decently and in order" (I Corinthians 14:40). And respect must be maintained for the older generation who did things differently. God is well honored and pleased in this.

The Lord will not stand by idle during the time of change either. He desires His will to be accomplished in the hearts of the people more than we do. His Holy Spirit will cause the hearts and minds of the people to be

TEAM MINISTRY

teachable and open to His direction and guidance (John 14:26). He will give confirmation of His will through the prophets:

> *Surely the Lord God will do nothing, but He revealeth His secret unto His servants the prophets. The lion hath roared, who will not fear? the Lord God hath spoken, who can but prophesy? (Amos 3:7-8)*

Change is possible by the power of the Holy Spirit, but it must be with forbearance, patience, and tenderness. We must be careful not to go ahead of the Lord.

IV. CHOOSING THE ELDERS

Choosing the elders for a local church that is beginning to establish a team ministry, is more difficult than finding elders in a church that is already operating under a team ministry. Here I would like to set forth a procedure for choosing and publicly recognizing new elders.

Prayer. The word church is derived from the Middle English word "kirke" which originated from the Greek kyriakos. This word is translated "belonging to the Lord." In truth the church belongs to the Lord. It is the Lord's church. He is to be recognized as Lord over His church. It belongs to Him.

> *And I will set up one shepherd over them, and he shall feed them, even my servant David; he shall feed them, and he shall be their shepherd. (Ezekiel 34:23)*

> *Who hath delivered us from the power of darkness, and hath translated us into the kingdom of His dear Son...and He is the head of the body, the church...(Colossians 1:13,18)*

> *Neither as being lords over God's heritage, but being ensamples to the flock. And when the chief Shepherd shall appear, you shall receive a crown of glory that fadeth not away. (I Peter 5:3-4)*

As Lord, He sovereignly determines who is going to receive what grace-gifts, and when. He dispenses from the

ORGANIZATIONAL GUIDELINES

throne, according to His grace and His choosing, the various gifts to different individuals (Ephesians 4:7-13). Christ is Lord over all the gifts and callings. He determines according to His excellent counsel and foreknowledge who the public ministers and leaders in a local church are going to be. The fivefold ministry of elders is divinely appointed.

...but our sufficiency is of God; who also hath made us able ministers of the new testament...(II Corinthians 3:5-6)

And all things are of God, who hath reconciled us to Himself by Jesus Christ, and hath given to us the ministry of reconciliation. (II Corinthians 5:18)

Whereof I was made a minister, according to the gift of grace of God given unto me by the effectual working of His power. (Ephesians 3:7; see also Colossians 1:23)

And I thank Christ Jesus our Lord, who hath enabled me, for that He counted me faithful, putting me into the ministry. (I Timothy 1:12)

Whereunto I am appointed a preacher, and an apostle, and a teacher of the Gentiles. (II Timothy 1:11)

God sovereignly appoints elders into the ministry and care of His people. As such it is of utmost importance that we seek the mind of God in seeking out elders. We need to ask, "Whom do you have in mind, Lord?" The choosing of elders involves not an "executive search" like the world would carry out. It is a search for the mind and will of the Lord for the church. And needs to be backed up by much prayer and fasting:

And when they had ordained them elders in every church, and had prayed with fasting, they commended them to the Lord...(Acts 14:23)

As they ministered to the Lord, and fasted, the Holy Ghost said, Separate Me Barnabas and Saul for the work whereunto I have called them. And when they had fasted and prayed, and laid their hands on them, they sent them away. (Acts 13:2-3)

TEAM MINISTRY

Appointing elders in the first local churches was done with much prayer and fasting. Even recommissioning elders for a different, or expansion of, ministry involved much prayer and fasting. God knows what is best for His church. He also knows who is best for His church in a specific locality.

It is important to the well-being of the sheep that only those elders are appointed as God has chosen. Prayer should be offered not only by the present ministry, but also by the congregation. By praying, the church is honoring and showing respect for the Lordship of Christ and acknowledging His sovereignty in all matters.

Qualifications. There is a much used verse that states, "many are called but few are chosen" (Matthew 22:14). This idea may be applied to the ministry in that God may call many into the public ministry but few respond to that call with diligence to become "chosen vessels."

It is true that God is the one who chooses, appoints and determines who should be elders. But it is also true that many sell out that high calling for a mess of pottage. Instead of responding with faith and determination to "the call" into the ministry, they succumb to the allurements of the present age, a world of tinsel.

Many treat their calling as a sort of fatalism: whatever will happen will happen when it happens. Others dabble in it as if it were a hobby. Some use it for their own material gain. Still others manipulate the ministry as a con game for profit.

Because of these abuses of the calling, there are laid down in the New Testament certain qualifications for elders to achieve, before they can be recognized and placed into service.

The New Testament is replete with verses describing the various qualities that a leader should have. Many of these are summarized in two of the Epistles of Paul:

ORGANIZATIONAL GUIDELINES

I Timothy 3:1-7 and Titus 1:5-9. More will be said later about the developing of these characteristics in a mature elder. But here I would like to list them so we know what to look for in an elder when we are searching for one:

Moral Characteristics
Blameless
Sober
Of good behavior
Not given to wine
No striker (contentious)
Not greedy of money
Patient
Not a brawler
Not covetous
Of good report without
Not self-willed
Not soon angry
Just
Devout
Temperate

Domestic Characteristics
Husband of one wife
Given to hospitality
Rules own house well
Children in subjection
    not unruly

Leadership Characteristics
Vigilant
Able to teach
Not a novice, experienced
Lover of good men
Steadfast to the Word

By scanning this list, you can see that with all the personal, moral qualities listed, an elder must first be a man, a real man. His personal development and maturity is of utmost priority. Next, in a broader sphere of influence he must be in harmony at home; his family life must be in order. And then, lastly he must have developed those qualities that are needed for the broader sphere of ministry and leadership in the church setting.

In looking over your local congregation you may find several potential men who are definitely called into public ministry, but any premature setting into that ministry may be fatal to them and to the sheep they oversee. These qualifications listed by Paul are an insurance against shipwreck. The temptations that come in leadership

TEAM MINISTRY

positions are powerful. The immature, the novice, the inexperienced, and the careless are easy prey for the snare of the devil (I Timothy 3:7).

> *...Be thou an example of the believers, in word, in conversation, in charity, in spirit, in faith, in purity. Till I come, give attendance to reading, to exhortation, to doctrine. Neglect not the gift that is in thee...meditate upon these things; give thyself wholly to them; that thy profiting may appear to all.*
>
> *Take heed unto thyself, and unto the doctrine; continue in them: for in doing this thou shalt both save thyself, and them that hear thee.*
> *(I Timothy 4:12-16)*

Consequently, prayer to discern those whom God has called, and then examining them to see if they have diligently developed and given heed to that calling, is essential.

Time. The "looking-over" process takes time. Team ministry is not something that can be rushed into. The examining of people's actions and character involves watching them in their daily practices. That takes time.

It's like a courtship and marriage. Two people are going to spend the rest of their lives in an intimate relationship, working together, facing a multitude of circumstances. But first, there must be a knitting of their hearts. A strong friendship must be developed. A loyalty and trust relationship must be fostered. Then comes marriage. One usually doesn't marry the first girl he meets. It takes time.

Neither does one hastily "put in a team" to run a church. Quick choices prove to be disastrous. "Well, we've got to have a team. So you all be on the team." That is the worst thing you can do. After awhile you find out that some of them have character flaws. Or, they do not have the same vision. Or, they are not really serious about their calling, not really dedicated to serving.

ORGANIZATIONAL GUIDELINES

In a courtship prior to marriage, two people consider if they want to walk in the same direction, speak the same thing, have the same goals. And agree on the same paths to achieve those goals. If they agree in these areas, then they feel confident to get married.

The same principle applies to choosing elders for your specific local church. You must spend time together. You oversee their activities in the sheepfold. You discern their compassion for the sheep by their self-sacrifice. Because, as working partners, you must have a trusting friendship, a relaxed confidence in each other.

Henceforth I call you not servants; for the servant knoweth not what his lord doeth: but I have called you friends; for all things that I have heard of my Father I have made known to you. (John 15:15)

You must have faith in others enough to delegate responsibilities to them. And that faith is based on friendships which are patiently developed.

A lumberyard is not equivalent to a house. The ingredients are the same. But one vital thing is missing. In one case, they are not fitted together. Several ministers thrown together in a local church do not constitute a team ministry. The potential is there. But they must be "fitted" together in harmony and unity of spirit and singleness of purpose. When you have this, then you have team ministry.

It seems from reading Acts 14:21-23 that Paul and Barnabas ordained elders in the newly started churches, not on their first, but during their second trip through the area. There was a short time period for the new converts to prove themselves in their diligence to make their calling and election sure.

V. ORDAINING THE ELDERS

After there has been much prayer, evaluation of prospective ministers, and time, then comes the actual selection and ordination of the elders. To understand this procedure it is important that we comprehend the word "ordain." The King James Version uses this word for translating ten different Greek words! Five of these are considered in some detail in Table 5, on page 93.

There seems to be both a divine and a human element in ordination. Primarily, it is the Lord who "sets, puts, appoints, commits, makes, or ordains" men into the ministry (that is, the public or leadership ministry).

The human participation seems to be the "recognition" of the divine appointments, and a commending to God's grace and care those so appointed. God ordains, but the elders with the congregation ratify that call publicly, acknowledging the maturity of the new elder. The church is consenting to the fact of that person's diligence in making his calling sure.

Ordination, then, is the public recognition of a grace-gift already bestowed by the Lord. It does not involve a "transfer of power." Nor does it involve "apostolic succession." It is simply an acknowledgement of authority previously given by God. The Lord is Lord of His church. He promotes whom He wills (Psalm 75:6-7).

It is good to point out that in the New Testament there is no ecclesiastical authority, other than God, higher than the local church. There is no outside hierarchial system that appoints elders or pastors to a local church.

The autonomy of the local church, with the mind of the Spirit, is everywhere recognized. The only obvious exception seems to be the cases where new, pioneer churches were started. The apostles, or their fellow laborers, organized and maintained discipline--ruled, if you please--the new churches until local Christians had matured as potential elders. Then they ordained local elders to carry on the work of the ministry.

TABLE 5

FIVE GREEK WORDS REPRESENTING ORDINATION

1. *kathistemi*   "appoint as ruler"

Titus 1:5 "*ordain* elders"
Acts 6:3 "*appoint* over this business"
Hebrews 2:7 "*set* him over the works of Thy hands"
Matthew 24:45 "*made ruler* over his household"
Hebrews 7:28 "*maketh* men high priests"
(See also Hebrews 5:1; 8:3).

2. *poieo*   "make, commit, do, cause, keep"

Mark 3:14 "*He ordained* twelve, that they should be with Him, and that He might send them forth to preach"

3. *tithemi*   "appoint, make, lay down, set, put"

I Timothy 2:7 "*ordained* a preacher"
John 15:16 "*ordained* you, that ye should bring forth fruit"
II Corinthians 5:19 "*committed* unto us the word of reconciliation"
Acts 13:47 "*set* thee to be a light of the Gentiles"
I Corinthians 12:18 "*set* the members every one of them in the body"
I Corinthians 12:28 "*set* some in the church, first apostles, secondarily prophets . . ."
II Timothy 1:11 "*appointed* a preacher"
I Timothy 1:12 "Christ . . . *putting* me into the ministry"

4. *cheirotoneo*   "ordain, choose"

Acts 14:23 "*ordained* them elders in every church"
II Corinthians 8:19 "*chosen* of the churches to travel with us"

5. *ginomai*   "be done, be made to be"

Acts 1:22 "must one be *ordained* to be a witness with us of His resurrection"

TEAM MINISTRY

For this cause left I thee in Crete, that thou shouldest set in order the things that are wanting, and ordain elders in every city, as I had appointed thee. (Titus 1:5)

Because of this, it is a good rule not to send away for an elder or pastor. A person should have been in the local congregation for at least one or two years before any consideration of eldership. He must know the sheep. And he must be known by the sheep. Christ laid down this vital principle and we must follow it clearly (John 10:14). No man, and especially men who must meet the rigid qualifications for spiritual eldership, can be adequately and properly evaluated in a one-week visit, or a trial sermon, or a board review. As previously stated this important step takes time.

If an experienced minister, an ex-pastor, or seminary graduate comes into the local church, he should serve the people as an ordinary member for at least a year, before any consideration for public ministry. God loves His flock. He gave His son for them in death. He does not want to see any of the sheep hurt. Safeguards like this are a step in the right direction to maintain that loving care.

VI. PRIESTHOOD OF BELIEVERS

The elders in a church, the team of ministers who are ordained, are not a "spiritual caste" nor are they to be considered an elite autonomous ruling body sent from some external hierarchy. Their authority is derived from the "priesthood of all believers":

...to the strangers scattered throughout Pontus, Galatia, Cappadocia, Asia and Bithynia...ye also, as lively stones, are built up a spiritual house, an holy priesthood, to offer up spiritual sacrifices...ye are a chosen generation, a royal priesthood, an holy nation, a peculiar people...(I Peter 1:1; 2:5,9)

And hath made us kings and priests unto God and His Father; to Him be glory and dominion for ever and ever. Amen. (Revelation 1:6)

ORGANIZATIONAL GUIDELINES

But ye shall be named the Priests of the Lord: men shall call you the Ministers of our God...(Isaiah 61:6)

And ye shall be unto me a kingdom of priests, and an holy nation...(Exodus 19:6)

The priesthood of the public ministry must be continually regarded as arising from the priesthood of the whole body of believers. There is no clergy-laity division in regard to the priesthood as in other religions. The Christian elder is to be considered a priest because he is a representative and spokesman for a priestly race. Our team of elders are not a separate "spiritual estate" but they are servants of the whole priestly congregation. Therefore I again emphasize, in team ministry, elders must come up through the ranks of the local church assembly, rather than from an outside power structure.

Nor does the public ministry (also called enabling ministry, Ephesians 4:12, ordained ministry, full time ministry) stand in opposition to the general ministry of all believers. There is no difference in essence. They are all priests. There is a difference only in roles and function in the body. Everyone in the church is to find their ministry and accomplish God's will for their life by fulfilling that ministry. The congregation does not support the clergy so that the clergy can do its job. Rather the elders enable the congregation to come to maturity in ministry so the church can be the church.

In the Jewish synagogue and in the early Christian church it is apparent that the ordaining of elders was performed by the existing elders with the consent of the congregation. The new elders were formally set apart to their ministry by elders already in office in the local church, usually during a religious service or ceremony.

The voice of the people and the discernment of the elders

The congregation in the church, as was also the custom in

TEAM MINISTRY

the synagogue, knew those who were to be appointed. They had a voice in suggesting or nominating possible choices. This was done in choosing the apostle to take Judas' place (Acts 1:23); in the selection of deacons (Acts 6:3); as well as in major decision-making (Acts 15:22). There was an active cooperation between elders and people.

In the final choice of the new elder, the Scriptures seem to indicate that the mind of the Spirit, or the prophetic and apostolic unction, determined the appointment. In the approving of the new apostle to take Judas' place, the eleven apostles cast lots. This was the ancient Biblical way of determining the will of God. God was making the choice.

And they prayed, and said, Thou, Lord, which knowest the hearts of all men, shew whether of these two Thou hast chosen. (Acts 1:24)

The nominations of the multitude in the selection of deacons were sent to the elders.

Whom they set before the apostles: and when they had prayed, they laid their hands on them. (Acts 6:6)

Prayer, that is, petitioning the Lord, to find His will was done first. Then hands were laid upon them. In his letter to Titus, Paul instructed Titus to appoint or ordain elders:

For this cause I left thee in Crete, that thou shouldest set in order the things that are wanting, and ordain elders in every city, as I had appointed thee. (TItus 1:5)

The Greek word used here for "ordain" is kathistemi, and has the connotation of appointing one as a ruler (see Table 5, page 93). Titus, whom Paul respected as an able minister of the Gospel (II Corinthians 8:16), seems to have been the instrument in finding the mind of the Spirit, and

ORGANIZATIONAL GUIDELINES

settling on the final choices. In the last example, Paul and Barnabas chose elders for the newly established churches during their first missionary journey.

And when they had ordained them elders in every church, and had prayed with fasting, they commended them to the Lord, on whom they believed. (Acts 14:23)

The apostles, the planters of the seedling congregation (I Corinthians 3:6), seem to have given final approval of the new elders. They chose them, undoubtedly, after having the mind of the Spirit. The group of men from whom Barnabas and Paul were chosen were prophets and teachers (Acts 13:1).

I think it is important that those making the final decision in the choice of elder, are men with the prophetic mantle. They will know what the Spirit is saying to the church. According to the New Testament, the spiritual elders are best qualified to make this decision, due to their calling and anointing.

Notice that the Greek word for "ordain" in this verse is cheirotoneo (see Table 5 on page 93). In studying the history of this word, it originally meant "choosing by a showing of the hands." But scholars consider the meaning of the word, as Luke used it, to simply be "appointing or choosing" without the voting implications. Words change their meanings with the passage of time (or in different cultures or generations). Thus for example, the word "prevent" in Old English meant to go before; but in the twentieth century it basically means to hinder or keep from occurring. Because of the origin of this word some churches consider this a precedent for "congregational voting," where the majority rules.

However, grammatically the sentence in Greek refers to the apostles doing the choosing, or voting. The subject is Paul and Barnabas. With their prophetic insight they confirmed God's choice of elders.

TEAM MINISTRY

The choosing of elders is not a majority proposition (absolute democracy), where the will of man reigns. It is the mind of the Spirit evidenced by a unity of conviction on the part of the whole congregation to accept the Lord's promotions (John 1:13).

The congregation and the elders together, in the unity of the Spirit, with much prayer and fasting, facilitate the selection of new elders. These new elders are to arise from out of the congregation. The congregation is to "know" their elder (John 10:14). It is from within the congregation that the new elder is to have served faithfully and has been proven (II Corinthians 8:22; I Timothy 5:19-20). It is also the prophetic unction, the scrutiny of the Holy Spirit, and the will of the Lord that is to confirm the setting in of new ministers. The final verdict: "It seemed good to the Holy Ghost and to us" (Acts 15:28).

On a very practical level, a dedicated new minister needs no nomination. His reputation precedes him because of the good report he has through his service and faithfulness. His good deeds speak loudly of his calling. News of his love for the sheep spreads throughout the flock.

As a safeguard, some churches require a three to six month probationary period before a person is set in by the laying on of hands. His tentative eldership is announced, and anyone knowing of any reason why he should not be ordained has opportunity to express in written form any serious reservation.

VII. LAYING ON OF HANDS

When the probationary period is over, the candidate is formally set into the office of ministry by "the laying on of hands."

When the Levites were consecrated for service in the tabernacle, the children of Israel were to lay their hands

ORGANIZATIONAL GUIDELINES

upon them (Numbers 8:10). Moses laid his hand upon Joshua when transferring his leadership to him (Numbers 27:18; Deuteronomy 34:9).

In the early church, hands were laid upon the newly appointed deacons (Acts 6:6). Also when ministers were commissioned with a new work, or a thrust into a new direction of labor, they had hands laid upon them (Acts 13:3). And men had hands laid upon them when they were given their ministerial grace-gift.

> But the Lord said unto him, Go thy way: for he is a chosen vessel unto Me, to bear My name before the Gentiles, and kings, and the children of Israel: for I will shew him how great things he must suffer for My name's sake. And Ananias went his way, and entered into the house; and putting his hands on him said, Brother Saul...(Acts 9:15-17)

> Neglect not the gift that is in thee, which was given thee by prophecy, with the laying on of the hands of the presbytery. (I Timothy 4:14)

> Wherefore I put thee in remembrance that thou stir up the gift of God, which is in thee by the putting on of my hands. (II Timothy 1:6)

The laying on of hands is a solemn ceremony symbolizing the imposition of delegated authority from the Lord. It represents formally the serious call to rule over His flock by example in word and deed. It sets in those who are commissioned by God to execute justice and righteousness in discipline in His body:

> And I will give unto thee the keys of the kingdom of heaven: and whatsoever thou shalt bind on earth shall be bound in heaven: and whatsoever thou shalt loose on earth shall be loosed in heaven. (Matthew 16:19; see also 18:18)

> Whose soever sins ye remit (forgive), they are remitted (forgiven) unto them; and whose soever sins ye retain, they are retained. (John 20:23)

The laying on of hands is the consummation or final act of placing into office (ordaining) those men who are to feed the flock of God by taking the oversight (I Peter 5:2).

PART SEVEN

Maintaining the long-range benefits of team ministry

There is an unwritten law that states that honeymoons can't last forever. After the wedding vows are spoken, after the organist finishes the love song, after the candles are snuffed out, after the excitement of the honeymoon wanes, then comes the stark reality that performing the wedding vows is going to take some doing.

In order to fulfill the goals that the two lovers carefully planned, they must now begin to make some adjustments, face unexpected obstacles, and learn the secrets of maintaining long-range communication.

A husband-wife team requires work and persistence if it is going to enjoy the maximum success that in early years was envisioned.

This is also true of team ministry! A successful ministry to the flock by a team of elders requires a dedication which is predicated upon a willingness to work at it. "Blood, sweat, and tears" was a motto that Sir Winston Churchill used to rally the people together during a time of stress. I'm sure the Apostle Paul would have used it as well, if he had thought of it first.

A ministerial team to be effective and productive and maintain peak performance over the years, must cultivate several essential qualities.

I. CULTIVATE COMMUNICATION LINES

Members of a team must maintain a line of open communication at all times. This is vital. There is a sense of awe when one sees a "slam dunk" in basketball. It is

MAINTAINING LONG-RANGE BENEFITS

made possible by the precise execution of moves which were the result of subtle gestures of communication between alert players. A nod of the head, a secret hand gesture, a quick vocal expression, and each of them knows what his next move is going to be. A team functions in this way because they have spent hours together, getting to know each other.

So also a team of elders must establish and maintain times spent together. Elders should meet no less than once a week with each other. This is important to keep informed on issues, needs, operations, developments and sudden emergencies. It is also significant since it reflects how each is going to respond to these issues, developments and emergencies. It is of top priority for senior elders to talk to the rest of the elders.

Henceforth I call you not servants; for the servant knoweth not what his lord doeth: but I have called you friends; for all things that I have heard of My Father I have made known to you. (John 15:15)

It does little good to have a team and then not communicate as a team. The team must share through communication the issues that face the ministry. The more communication there is, the more "slam dunks" and victories there will be. The ability to verbalize and explain complex situations cuts large problems down to size. It can turn mountains into molehills.

Not only must there be communication between elders, but the team of elders must maintain communication with the people. The problem of rebuilding Jerusalem was facilitated by Nehemiah's capacity to clearly lay the needs before the people, as well as the rulers and nobles.

And the rulers knew not whither I went, or what I did; neither had I as yet told it to the Jews...nor to the rest that did the work. Then said I unto them, Ye see the distress that we are in...Then I told them of the

TEAM MINISTRY

hand of my God which was good upon me...And they said, Let us rise up and build. So they strengthened their hands for this good work. (Nehemiah 2:16-18)

The early church is noted for its open communication between its elders and the people. Matters of importance and those steps necessary to be taken were freely shared, and general concurrence was apparent:

And when they were come, and had gathered the church together, they rehearsed all that God had done with them...(Acts 14:27)

Then pleased it the apostles and elders, with the whole church, to send chosen men of their own company to Antioch...(Acts 15:22; see also 15:3,12,30)

For I verily, as absent in body, but present in spirit, have judged already...in the name of our Lord Jesus Christ, when we are gathered together, and my spirit, with the power of our Lord Jesus Christ, to deliver such an one unto Satan...(I Corinthians 5:3-5)

Moreover if thy brother shall trespass against thee, go and tell him his fault between thee and him alone: if he shall hear thee, thou hast gained thy brother. But if he will not hear thee, then take with thee one or two more, that in the mouth of two or three witnesses every word may be established. And if he shall neglect to hear them, tell it unto the church...(Matthew 18:15-17)

Such openness keeps a high level of trust and confidence among the people of the local church. Candor and frankness are all the more important during times of stress, change, or sudden developments.

II. KEEP BIBLICAL VISION IN PERSPECTIVE

As elders, it is also important to see our roles within the total perspective of the church. All believers are members of the priesthood in the kingdom of God. It is the duty of the elders to rule, feed, and train believers in order to bring them to maturity so they can properly function as priests.

MAINTAINING LONG-RANGE BENEFITS

And He gave some apostles and some, prophets; and some, evangelists; and some, pastors and teachers; for the perfecting of the saints, for the work of the ministry...(Ephesians 4:11-12)

We must never lose sight of this vision, or goal. This is our objective. We are to mature the sheep away from dependency on us so that truly they can say, "The Lord is my shepherd" (Psalm 23:1). We will have done our job well if we have worked ourselves out of a job. Each member needs to learn to hear the Shepherd's voice. Each needs to be able to receive guidance from Him. Each needs to learn to do His bidding when He calls to them. And each needs to minister to others in His strength.

Now I realize we elders won't really work ourselves totally out of a job because there will always be new young lambs coming into the church that will need maturing. But the "old sheep" should be becoming mature in Christian service or something is wrong. The goal is not to have the people dependent upon the pastor so that "we just can't do with out the pastor." That kind of statement may build up a pastor's ego. But it also reveals a failure to maintain the vision that the Bible places before elders.

...Christ in you, the hope of glory: Whom we preach, warning every man, and teaching every man in all wisdom; that we may present every man perfect in Christ Jesus. (Colossians 1:27-28)

...always labouring fervently for you in prayers, that ye may stand perfect and complete in all the will of God. (Colossians 4:12)

By maintaining this vision, the elders lessen the danger of becoming a spiritual clique, a dictatorial oligarchy, or even something worse. The Biblical purpose for having elders must be continually kept before us: mature the sheep for ministry.

A church that is growing and is placing its own people in new leadership roles is displaying the fact that it has

TEAM MINISTRY

discovered this Biblical principle and is fulfilling it faithfully. A church that sends out some of its elders and its people to start new churches is proving that it has maintained the correct vision. Its people are mature for service in the kingdom.

III. ENCOURAGE DIVERSITY AND VARIETY

The New Testament clearly teaches that there are many different gifts which God through Jesus Christ has given to the church (I Corinthians 12; Romans 12). The strength of a team of elders is in this unique diversity and variety. But how easy it is for a team to lapse into conformity. Conformity is a subtle force which increases its pressure with time. Just as water seeks the lowest level so the desire to conform drags a team down.

Each elder is unique and therefore cannot conform to a set mold. He must recognize his unique gift with which he is to serve the body. He needs to examine his limitations, his strengths and weaknesses. Eldership assignments must be matched to this uniqueness. The senior elder must keep an eye out and oversee so that the right person is in the right place doing the right job with the right gift. Proper coordination makes for a smooth-working team.

A word of caution is in order here. When a need arises in a certain area or department, some churches write out a job description listing all the needed requirements for that position. The problem is that seldom can one man meet all those requirements. Consequently, the person chosen has the unhappy duty of trying to "wear a shoe that doesn't quite fit." Because of this, job descriptions should be made to fit the man and his unique gift and abilities, rather than vice versa. You can still have guidelines, concrete goals, expectations; but they are to be reasonable and within the limitations of the grace measured out to the specific person.

MAINTAINING LONG-RANGE BENEFITS

IV. ALLOW FOR MARGINS

A word that dominates the Epistles of Paul, a man who worked in the ministry with several teams, is the word "grace" (Romans 1:5; 16:24; I Corinthians 1:3; 16:23; II Corinthians 1:2; 13:14; Galatians 1:3; 6:18; Ephesians 1:2; 6:18; Philippians 1:2; 4:23; Colossians 1:2; 4:18; I Thessalonians 1:1).

Paul opened and closed his letters with "grace." And the oil that will make a team function smoothly is this grace. You must allow for mistakes, even to the point of ignoring them, unless they are consistently the same kind of error.

Give each other latitude. Allow for margins.

An elder is not supposed to be a novice. That rule must be maintained. But elders make mistakes, too. And we must give each other the freedom to fail, now and then. Love "hopeth all things" (I Corinthians 13:7). It is proper to reserve judgment on a fellow elder in a matter until all the pertinent facts are known. Be gracious:

Brethren, if a man be overtaken in a fault, ye which are spiritual, restore such an one in the spirit of meekness; considering thyself, let thou also be tempted. Bear ye one another's burdens, and so fulfil the law of Christ. (Galatians 6:1-2)

A good, healthy sense of humor can do wonders when one goofs. Being gracious, laughing it off, allowing for margins helps a struggling elder maintain his stride. It encourages resiliency, and helps him "bounce back" with renewed determination. Grace is love in action.

V. SET THE PACE IN PERSONAL GROWTH

In several of his letters the Apostle Paul speaks of abounding more and more.

TEAM MINISTRY

And this I pray, that your love may abound yet more and more in knowledge and in all judgment. (Philippians 1:9)

Furthermore then we beseech you, brethren, and exhort you by the Lord Jesus, that as ye have received of us how ye ought to walk and to please God, so ye would abound more and more. (I Thessalonians 4:1)

...but we beseech you, brethren, that ye increase more and more. (I Thessalonians 4:10; see also 3:12)

There is nothing more detrimental to an organization, program or institution than for it to be overseen by a group of men who hold to antiquated methods, outdated ideas, or outmoded skills. It stymies progress and inhibits growth.

The church is alive! And it is decreed that it must grow. ("The gates of hell shall not prevail against it" Matthew 16:18.)

This means that the elders must set the example in growing continually. Each must keep his professional skills sharp. Each must inspire the others to the highest professional standards. Each needs to encourage the other to abound more and more in his gift and calling:

Wherefore I put thee in remembrance that thou stir up the gift of God, which is in thee by the putting on of my hands. (II Timothy 1:6)

This growth involves spiritual measures that must be taken. But it also involves some practical steps. An elder may attend a seminar, take a refresher course, or sit in on a continuing education class. Some churches feel it vitally necessary to hold their own "Elders' Training Sessions" regularly. However it is done, the elders on a team must stay informed, improve areas of weaknesses, and develop greater strengths.

Ministerial workshops and conferences are an excellent way to improve skills, not only because of new knowledge and information that may be gleaned, but there a team can

MAINTAINING LONG-RANGE BENEFITS

meet with other teams to discuss issues and ideas. Sharing experiences of real-life situations is a tremendous benefit to growth.

There is some debate as to how much technology can be employed in the church without losing the personal warmth of the Gospel. But no one can doubt the importance of the printed page nor of the cassette tape.

The kingdom of God does benefit from judicious use of modern technologies. Elders do well to stay informed and keep up with efficient ways of reaching more people with the Gospel.

In short, the elders must be pacesetters in personal growth.

VI. BE SENSITIVE TO OTHERS' NEEDS

Be sensitive to the needs of each other on the team. You may be professional men. But you are also human beings with physical needs, financial problems, family demands and social desires. Check up on each other in these areas.

Look not every man on his own things, but every man also on the things of others. (Philippians 2:4)

Elders not only share in the vision and goals of the church, they have personal goals as well. Occasionally you need to ask each other, "How can I help you reach God's goals for your life?" In order to do this with sincerity you are going to have to get to know each other, in a close relationship. This is not only achieved by regular, formal elders' business meetings; but also through times of social gatherings. It is good for elders to have recreation together, or for their families to go on picnics together.

Most ministers abuse their bodies. This abuse leads to premature death, or emotional burnout. The odd hours, stressful counselling, hours of sitting dealing with the financial problems of the church, missed meals, all of these

TEAM MINISTRY

can take their toll on the health of the minister. It's important to tell each other: relax. Don't take yourself too seriously.

Elders should take time out for some physical exercise together. A lot of problems can be solved while relaxing in a sauna. And much enlightenment can come to me while leaning over a tennis net. The fresh outdoors can stimulate new ideas and provide exciting creativity to clergical duties.

A minister also has domestic problems that are unique to his profession. What a lifesaver it is for another minister to pick up on your family need and make suggestions that he and his family implemented successfully. Children of ministers can be some of the most neglected people in the church. Elders can provide an immense service by exhorting each other to spend more time with the kids. Most fathers--no matter how hard they have tried--say, after looking back: "I should have spent more time with my kids." It is good at times to have retreats for the elders' families; sharing meals together, playing together and praying together.

A team that does not exploit each other for their own personal ambitions and goals, but rather shares in each other's goals and is sensitive to each other's needs cannot but help attain peak performance in the ministry. This empathy for one another was demonstrated by Paul toward his team members:

Yet I supposed it necessary to send to you Epaphroditus, my brother, and companion in labour, and fellow soldier, but your messenger, and he that ministered to my wants. For indeed he was sick nigh unto death: but God had mercy on him; and not on him only, but on me also, lest I should have sorrow upon sorrow. (Philippians 2:25,27)

To Timothy...I thank God...that without ceasing I have remembrance of thee in my prayers night and day; greatly desiring to see thee, being mindful of thy tears, that I may be filled with joy. (II Timothy 1:2-4)

MAINTAINING LONG-RANGE BENEFITS

I beseech thee for my son Onesimus...whom I would have retained with me, that in thy stead he might have ministered unto me in the bonds of the gospel...receive him for ever; not now as a servant, but above a servant, a brother beloved, specially to me...If he hath wronged thee, or oweth thee aught, put that on mine account. (Philemon 1:10,13,15-16,18)

With compassion and sensitivity like that, no doubt anyone would have considered it a privilege to work alongside Paul in the ministry.

VII. LEARN HOW TO LISTEN

No matter how much you think the team depends upon you, and no matter how much you have contributed to the team in the past, it is mandatory to keep a listening ear open to the other elders. They hear from God as well as you. If you are a senior elder, stay humble and listen to the other team members. If you are at an important time of decision, one of them may just have the key needed for that hour. Give attention to all they are saying and prayerfully consider it. Don't ever belittle suggestions, even those from your weakest member. Your attitude should be "I don't care who makes the touchdown. We are a team!"

Solicit opinions. Ask questions. Encourage suggestions. We all want to work smarter, not longer.

Bow down thine ear, and hear the words of the wise...(Proverbs 22:17)

Keep thy foot when thou goest to the house of God, and be more ready to hear, than to give...Be not rash with thy mouth, and let not thine heart be hasty to utter anything before God: for God is in heaven, and thou upon earth: therefore let thy words be few. (Ecclesiastes 5:1-2)

Incline your ear, and come unto me: hear, and your soul shall live...(Isaiah 55:3)

...unto you that hear shall more be given. (Mark 4:24)

Wherefore, my beloved brethren, let every man be swift to hear, slow to speak...(James 1:19)

TEAM MINISTRY

Receiving ideas from others is a safeguard against pride. We cannot say our wisdom and might has accomplished this or that. We received from one another. Even Christ did not speak only from Himself. He humbled Himself and spoke only that which He heard from His Father:

> *For I have not spoken of Myself; but the Father which sent Me, He gave Me a commandment, what I should say, and what I should speak...whatsoever I speak therefore, even as the Father said unto Me, so I speak. (John 12:49-50)*

In the same way, the Holy Spirit does not speak only from Himself. He speaks to us from that which He hears.

> *Howbeit when He, the Spirit of truth, is come, He will guide you into all truth: for He shall not speak of Himself; but whatsoever He shall hear, that shall He speak...(John 16:13)*

If two members of the Trinity give attendance to listening, it is not unreasonable for elders to learn to listen also. They are to listen to God, the Father; God, the Son; and God, the Holy Spirit; to God's Word; to each other; and may we add, to the people also.

All the elders on the team should be given a chance to be heard on any given topic. The rest are to listen.

In Acts 15 we have a good illustration of this. James, the senior elder at the Jerusalem church, led the discussion on a very important doctrinal issue. He listened to what various ones had to say, including Peter and Paul, before he made his judgment on the subject.

VIII. ESTEEM ONE ANOTHER AS EQUALS

Each team member must be allowed to feel that he is a vital member of the team. He is an associate. Not an assistant. You are all co-laborers, subject to one another

MAINTAINING LONG-RANGE BENEFITS

in mutual submission (I Peter 5:5; Ephesians 5:21). Each must remain impartial toward the others, treating all elders alike. There should be no favoritism nor discrimination. No attitude or mental posture must be allowed to inhibit the full contribution of each of the elders to the decisions that need to be made, and to the full work of the ministry.

It was Paul's custom to esteem, show gratitude, recognize and fully appreciate each of his yokefellows in the Gospel (Philippians 4:3).

> *And we beseech you, brethren, to know them which labour among you, and are over you in the Lord, and admonish you; and to esteem them very highly in love for their work's sake...*
> *(I Thessalonians 5:12-13)*
>
> *Let nothing be done through strife or vainglory; but in lowliness of mind let each esteem other better than themselves. (Philippians 2:3)*

This mutual respect shows up in the congregation. We must give honor to all the team members if they are to have leadership influence in the body. If the elders do not show equal respect among themselves how will the people respect them as leaders.

> *And the Lord said unto Moses, Take thee Joshua the son of Nun.....and set him before Eleazar the priest, and before all the congregation; and give him a charge in their sight. And thou shalt put some of thine honour upon him, that all the congregation of the children of Israel may be obedient. (Numbers 27:18-20)*

No one member, no single clique, is to aspire to dominate the team. The twelve apostles succumbed to this error:

> *And there was also a strife among them, which of them should be accounted the greatest. (Luke 22:24; see also Mark 9:34 and Luke 9:46)*
>
> *...Grant that these my two sons may sit, the one on Thy right hand, and the other on the left, in Thy kingdom. (Matthew 20:21)*

TEAM MINISTRY

The early church was plagued with the same tendency:

I wrote unto the church: but Diotrephes, who loveth to have the preeminence among them, receiveth us not. (III John 9)

No one elder is to strive for popularity over the others. Neither is one to compete with another. This is why we suggest each elder is not to develop a fleshly, platform personality. This not only involves attitude but also conduct in dress. The elders should all dress moderately, not calling attention to themselves by their apparel.

Power corrupts the best of leaders and it has been said that "absolute power corrupts absolutely." We are simply to seek to serve the people of God with humility, esteeming the other better than ourselves (I Corinthians 1:26-31).

Take time out to show appreciation to your fellow laborer by a note, a gift, a word, or an evening together. Encourage them privately and praise them publicly. Give credit where credit is due. Demonstrate pride in them. This brings out their best. Leaders usually receive more than their share of the blame and less than their share of the credit. It is sweet music to their ears to hear a word of appreciation now and then, and more likely than not they deserve more than they are getting.

Nehemiah showed his keenness of insight as a leader in the third chapter of his book. There he listed by name all the people who were in charge of repairing each section of the wall. By listing these men he was giving them commendation for work well done. Now, thousands of years later, we can still read their names, and honor them for their courage and stamina in rebuilding the city during times of opposition and peril.

Give honor to whom honor is due, preferring one another (I Peter 2:17; Romans 12:10; 13:7) remembering that elders are "worthy of double honor" (I Timothy 5:17).

114

MAINTAINING LONG-RANGE BENEFITS

IX. GIVE ROOM FOR CREATIVITY

When an elder is assigned to oversee a department of the church, allow him flexibility. Give him room to carry out that duty. A job description is all right if it centers on the final objective, but not on the method or way the job is carried out.

The team of elders is not merely a group of "yes men" carrying out the orders of the senior elder. Warning signs that this is happening are when they ask such questions every day or so, as "Now what?" "What do you want me to do now?" "What's next on the agenda?" Do not rob fellow elders of motivation by stifling their creativity with too many directives.

Many leaders groan inside because they are not allowed to use all the talents, gifts and abilities God has placed within them. You have all heard the famous last words: "We can't do it that way. We've never done it that way before." Do not force unnecessary traditions upon an elder's department. There is nothing wrong with fresh approaches to old ideas. This is not change for change's sake, but for life's sake.

In fact every program of the local church should be periodically evaluated and updated. If a program is not working, change it or drop it. Programs are to last as long as they work, and no longer. As a tree is known by its fruit, so every program needs to be evaluated on its results (Luke 6:44). Someone has said, "You get what you inspect, not what you expect."

For the updating, evaluating process to occur, the elder needs room for creativity. Let him think. Let some sparks fly. Let his brain crank out new ideas. Encourage his creativity by not being defensive of past methods.

An elder can find fulfillment in ministry if he's not treated like a robot or a puppet. Allow him freedom to explore alternatives; to make mistakes; to ask questions such as "Is there a better way?"

Then, guess what! He just might run across a better method. A cheaper process, a more time-effective way of meeting the goals in this area of responsibility. And everyone benefits when this happens. What's more he will have more enthusiasm for his work, be more optimistic.

Praise initiative. Exude excitement at another's discoveries. It will become infectious and expand your thinking as well. Help each other out. Suggest improvements and give reasons; learn to constructively criticize and to analyze. Learn to receive suggestions and to receive constructive analysis. In Biblical language, exhort one another to perfect each area of ministry for God's glory.

X. PRACTICE LOYALTY TO ONE ANOTHER

Team ministry requires a high standard of ethics, honesty, and integrity. Elders must be straightforward in dealing with their colleagues. Openness in discussion and freedom to disagree should be encouraged. But they are not to compete with each other. Rather, each should respect the position of authority in which they are placed. If weaknesses are discovered in a brother, they should be covered, and not exposed.

Disloyalty is usually suggested by subtle remarks or insinuations. "You preach better than the other elder." If you hear that enough times, you might be tempted to believe it. Then you begin to exalt yourself above your fellow elders. Then tragedy!

"The other elder said this when he rebuked me. Do you think that's fair?" Watch for this one. Don't allow people to play one elder against another. We have all seen children do this to their parents.

Nevertheless, handling this response requires extreme tactfulness. If what was said sounded really bad, then you should still respect the position of that elder. One might say: "I'm sure the elder had good reason to say what he did. For clarification, let us consult him." Usually the person is just looking for a way to avoid discipline. Don't join in with his murmuring.

> *...Murmur not among yourselves. (John 6:43)*

> *Only let your conversation be as it becometh the gospel of Christ: that whether I come and see you, or else be absent, I may hear of your affairs, that ye stand fast in one spirit, with one mind striving together for the faith of the gospel. (Philippians 1:27)*

> *Do all things without murmurings and disputings: that ye may be blameless and harmless, the sons of God...(Philippians 2:14-15)*

> *And Miriam and Aaron spake against Moses...Hath the Lord indeed spoken only by Moses?...and, behold, Miriam became leprous...(Numbers 12:1,2,10)*

Members of the team should learn to defer to the other members of the team when they are functioning in their area of authority. Even the senior pastor should have great respect for an elder's placement and not overrule him unless he genuinely feels that he is acting in the best interest of the church.

When there is disagreement in elders' meetings and a decision is ultimately reached, it is important to unitedly support the resolution in the presence of the people. After all, the next decision may go your way, with other elders still in disagreement, and you would want their support in front of the people.

When differences of opinion exist make an earnest effort to resolve them. Defend your principles and convictions even in the face of peer pressure. Make sure your position is based upon principle and maintain that position without considering its popularity or convenience until the final decision is reached by the team. Then support the team's decision.

TEAM MINISTRY

The writer of Genesis spoke of a man leaving his father and mother and of "cleaving" unto his wife (Genesis 2:24). The word "cleave" means "to cling to, to be faithful to." In team ministry, it might be symbolically appropriate to say that elders need to "cleave" to each other.

XI. WORK FOR A SPIRIT OF UNITY

For a team to work smoothly there must be a strong emphasis upon unity of spirit. Unity in diversity must be maintained.

> *Endeavoring to keep the unity of the Spirit in the bond of peace...Till we all come in the unity of faith, and of the knowledge of the Son of God...(Ephesians 4:3,13)*
>
> *...that ye all speak the same thing, and that there be no divisions among you; but that ye be perfectly joined together in the same mind and in the same judgment. (I Corinthians 1:10)*
>
> *...that ye stand fast in one spirit, with one mind striving together for the faith of the gospel. (Philippians 1:27)*
>
> *Fulfil ye my joy, that ye be likeminded, having the same love, being of one accord, of one mind. (Philippians 2:2)*

It is not enough to gather an orchestra of skilled musicians. It is not enough to have the correct number of players. It is not enough to distribute the same music. Each member must be in tune with each other and all of them in tune with the piano. Then you have a harmonious working relationship.

Unity is not necessarily uniformity. What is important is a spirit of unity. There can still be diverse gifts, diverse ideas and diverse opinions. It is how we handle those diversities that determines the effectiveness of the team. Disagreement is not the same as disunity. In fact, disagreement can be good when it forces a closer look at the issues. It compels a more serious consideration of all the facts. Conflict is normal and we are to expect it. But we are to "speak the truth in love" as we understand it to be (Ephesians 4:15).

The following guidelines may help maintain unity during times of discussion on important matters:

1. Examine all the alternatives to a situation. Look at the positive options. Don't give ultimatums which force a person into a corner.
2. Keep discussions impersonal. Ask "What is right?" not "Who is right?" This helps to keep it out of the realm of the emotions.
3. Switch roles and argue the other side. One must see the opposite view clearly to make a rational decision, an enlightened decision.
4. Don't judge motives or question the integrity of those with whom you disagree. Judge only judgments. Question only the proposals.
5. If the major, ultimate decision seems unattainable at the present, look for possible agreement on short term goals.
6. Keep the disagreement clean. Build decisions on the faith and hope that love is everyone's motivation.
7. Compromise is not a dirty word. When principles aren't involved, compromise can get the ball rolling. Be flexible and adjust.
8. Discern the right timing. The idea might be right, but the timing wrong. Wait. Put it on the shelf for a more appropriate day.

The New Testament church era is marked by several major disagreements on doctrine, method, tradition, personalities and conduct. But one cannot help but feel the earnest desire of all the apostles and disciples that unity of spirit and purpose in publishing the Gospel is maintained. Immediate consensus was encouraged.

It seemed good unto us, being assembled with one accord...For it seemed good to the Holy Ghost, and to us. (Acts 15:25,28)

TEAM MINISTRY

It was desired that nothing hinder the churches, nor harm the congregations. Problems were not ignored then, nor should they be brushed aside now. They are to be dealt with in the spirit of love which unifies all Christians.

XII. HOLD FORTH LOVING DISCIPLINE

Strong and loving discipline is the only way to maintain a pure example of the Christian life. And it is by example that elders are to rule. If one is called to be an elder, he is called to be an example.

> *Brethren, be followers together of me, and mark them which walk so as ye have us for an ensample.* (Philippians 3:17)
>
> *In all things showing thyself a pattern of good works: in doctrine shewing uncorruptness, gravity, sincerity.* (Titus 2:7)
>
> *Be ye followers of me, even as I also am of Christ.* (I Corinthians 11:1)
>
> *Neither as being lords over God's heritage, but being ensamples to the flock.* (I Peter 5:3)

The temptations for a minister to depart from "the example" are many. If Satan can corrupt the leaders, destroy the shepherds, then the sheep are easy prey. We must not be ignorant of his devices (II Corinthians 2:11). An elder must keep a guard on every aspect of his life:

1. *Mind*: The position of power that an elder may seem to have can corrupt his attitudes. Instead of humility, pride creeps in.

2. *Money:* Many preachers are poor. They are not skilled in handling large sums of money properly (large offerings). Other ministers who become prosperous are tempted to spend it where it is not allocated.

MAINTAINING LONG-RANGE BENEFITS

3. *Morals:* Counselling situations lend themselves to risky situations. Platform popularity adds to this delicate situation.

4. *Marriage:* Ministers may tend to ignore the needs of their wives. Their busy schedules often take them away from the children too much.

5. *Misgivings:* In any social work, it is hard to keep the job separate from personal emotions. Discouragement, bitterness and disillusionment are all part of the territory.

6. *Ministerial:* Ruling the Gentiles as lords is a common failure of ministers. Their is a temptation to become lawgivers, instead of ministers of grace. Leadership become cultic, bringing in false doctrines.

It is a sad thing to hear of a minister that has "gone bad." It is like hearing of a corrupt judge, or a policeman on the take. The whole scene is demoralizing. It causes some to lose faith in the whole man and his family.

Corruption influences the whole sphere of his job and all the people under his jurisdiction. For this reason Paul put forth strong guidelines to Timothy to enact in this type of situation:

> *Against an elder receive not an accusation, but before two or three witnesses. Them that sin rebuke before all, that others also may fear. I charge thee before God, and the Lord Jesus Christ, and the elect angels, that thou observe these things without preferring one before another, doing nothing by partiality. Lay hands suddenly on no man, neither be partaker of other men's sins: keep thyself pure. (I Timothy 5:19-22)*

TEAM MINISTRY

Discipline against a fallen elder is to be made public. But, as in all church discipline, the ultimate goal is restoration. Therefore it is to be done in love and meekness, for we are all subject to the same temptations (Galatians 6:1).

IN SUMMARY. How do we maintain the long-range benefits of team ministry? Well, in addition to the twelve essential qualities discussed here (and there are more), there is something beautiful about how team ministry provides a daily check and balance among the elders for each other.

By checking up on and encouraging each other, by submitting to each other, many a problem and sin can be nipped in the bud.

"How's your family doing?" "Are you fulfilling the needs of your wife?" "How's your prayer life, lately?" "How is it between you and the Lord?" "How are you doing financially? Need any help?" "Can I help you in budgeting?" "I've noticed a little bit of arrogance in you, can I pray with you?" "You seem disturbed, would you like to talk about it?" "Something seems to be bothering you. May I help you solve it?"

If each elder has a responsive heart to loving discipline, it will yield the peaceable fruit of righteousness (Hebrews 12:11).

Acknowledge, and take measures to correct them. And you will both save yourself and those that hear you (I Timothy 4:16).

Best of all, examples like this can be contagious. They can infect a whole congregation. And the members of the congregation, in turn, can benefit the communities in which they live--like salt and light benefit all of us.

PART EIGHT

Training new elders to form the leadership team

As with love and marriage, children and marriage also go together like a horse and carriage. Children are a natural and normal result of a healthy marriage relationship. And parents soon begin to realize that these children need training, teaching and discipline for proper growth and development. A large amount of time and money is spent fulfilling this new responsibility.

In team ministry, the training of new elders becomes critically important. In fact, the more effectively the elders function, the more inevitable becomes the growth and expansion of the membership in the local church.

New spiritual children just seem to spring up all over the place. And the goal of any eldership must be to train, teach and discipline these new members so that they might develop in their relationship to Jesus Christ, in their relationship to Jesus Christ, in their relationship to each other, and in their relationship to their own unique ministry in the body.

Some of these children, God will call (ordain) to the public ministry. Consequently, the development of new elders to serve a growing church is one of the most vital on-going aspects of a church's responsibilities. The growth and maturing of these spiritual elders is also one of the most rewarding and exciting developments in the church.

In this part, we will discuss nine guidelines to follow in developing new elders.

FORMING THE LEADERSHIP TEAM

I. EXPLORE GOD'S METHOD

First, it is important to keep in mind that the Lord is our Shepherd. We are to follow Him in all things. We are to follow His example in all programs, including the training and development of elders. The church is the Lord's. He watches over it jealously.

Because His thoughts are higher than our thoughts, we sometimes resort to Gentile thinking in training new elders. We have a propensity to follow the latest leadership-executive criterion developed in our university psychology departments. But team ministry is more than just the infusion of technological skills or academic achievements, it is vitally linked with character development and spiritual qualifications.

In the prophetic book of Isaiah, the Lord warns us that He will not give His glory to another (Isaiah 48:11; see also Jeremiah 9:23-24). This principle might well apply to the training of ministers. No man makes the church great. It is the Lord who blesses His church. There are good leaders in the church because the Lord has developed them for His ministry.

Abraham. The old patriarch, Abraham, recognized this principle. When the king of Sodom wanted to give him all the booty after a battle, Abraham replied:

> *I have lift up mine hand unto the Lord, the most high God, the possessor of heaven and earth, that I will not take from a thread even to a shoelatchet, and that I will not take anything that is thine, lest thou shouldest say, I have made Abram rich. (Genesis 14:22-23)*

The Lord watched over Abraham. Today, He watches over the development of His elders. And He will not share His glory with human methods of leadership training.

> *Except the Lord build the house, they labour in vain that build it: except the Lord keep the city, the watchman waketh but in vain. It is vain for you to rise up early, to sit up late, to eat the bread of sorrows: for so He giveth His beloved sleep. (Psalm 127:1-2)*

TEAM MINISTRY

Trusting the Lord. The Psalmist emphasized that the Lord is indeed watching over His house and knows just what it needs. It is vain to stay up worrying about anything because even while you are sleeping the Lord is busy supplying your need. What confidence and rest there is in following God's methods.

God is sovereign. He is sovereign in the affairs of a man. No man or demon can stop God from fulfilling His will in a new elder. Satan can't. Man can't. No one can stop whatever God wants to do in your life for good. That's exciting!

> *Lift not up your horn on high: speak not with a stiff neck. For promotion cometh neither from the east, nor from the west, nor from the south. But God is the judge: He putteth down one, and setteth up another. (Psalm 75:5-7)*

> *My soul, wait thou only upon God; for my expectation is from Him...God hath spoken once; twice have I heard this; that power belongeth unto God. Also unto Thee, O Lord, belongeth mercy: for Thou renderest to every man according to his work. (Psalm 62:5,11-12)*

Man's idea of development and promotion is usually based on self-centered strength, which often leads to pride. God's method of development and promotion is simply trusting Him. Promotion comes to the humble. It comes to those who let patience have its perfect work. It comes to those who recognize God's sovereignty in appointing times and seasons (Daniel 2:21).

As elders, it is our duty to point young ministers to the Lord and to teach them to submit to His sovereign school of ministerial development, to have confidence in God's ability to mature them, to recognize each circumstance as an opportunity for growth and to follow the Lord's methods of promotion only.

FORMING THE LEADERSHIP TEAM

II. EXPAND OUR HORIZONS

In order for us as elders to guide young men in their relationship with the Lord and His training methods, we first have to know whom God has chosen. Our immediate tendency is to run to the Bible college graduates. We tend to look over the most likely prospects--that is, the handsome, well-dressed, socially extroverted, and academically advanced individuals--and smile with approval at their many qualifications. And many of them do go on to be excellent ministers of the Word. Churches need to take advantage of the many Bible colleges, so that the church members can be thoroughly taught in Biblical education. The growth in the number of Bible colleges has shown a keen desire on the part of Christians to understand God's ways and works.

But God can do much more than that. He can enlarge our understanding of His ways. As elders, we need to be aware of the many areas of life in which God is patiently developing potential, young elders. Great men of God in the Bible suddenly appeared from many different unexpected segments of society. Abraham was a businessman. David was a shepherd. Peter was a fisherman. Moses was a statesman turned shepherd. And Nehemiah (an excellent leader) was a slave cupbearer.

Neither did they all come from well-adjusted, well-to-do families. Timothy was a half-breed. Moses was a foster child. Paul was hardly a likable character.

It seems to be a principle with God to champion the underdog. To lift up the poor and needy.

Who is like unto the Lord our God, who dwelleth on high, who humbleth Himself to behold the things that are in heaven, and in the earth! He raiseth up the poor out of the dust, and lifteth the needy out of the dunghill; that He may set him with princes, even with the princes of His people. (Psalm 113:5-8)

TEAM MINISTRY

God looks on the heart, the integrity and the character of individuals when He chooses spiritual leadership. He looks anywhere and everywhere:

> *For the eyes of the Lord run to and fro throughout the whole earth, to shew Himself strong in the behalf of them whose heart is perfect toward Him...(II Chronicles 16:9)*

Not only does God tend to look lower than we tend to look. He not only looks in more places than we tend to look. He also looks with a different kind of eye:

> *But the Lord said unto Samuel, Look not on his countenance, or on the height of his stature; because I have refused him: for the Lord seeth not as man seeth; for man looketh on the outward appearance, but the Lord looketh on the heart. (I Samuel 16:7)*

Being a mighty prophet of God did not prevent Samuel from making the mistake we too often make: we judge by appearance. Samuel was trying to outguess God. He assumed that the handsome one, or the intellectual one, or the most popular one would be the one that God would choose as the next king of Israel.

David's heart was right with God. He was a mighty man of integrity, faithful in the duties that were at hand. As elders we need to recognize that God looks on the heart. In seeking out new elders for development the foremost question in our minds should be "Lord, what is his heart like?" "Is his heart prepared for the task of the ministry?" "Is his heart pliable in Your hands?"

Teach the people God's ways. We also should teach not only the potential leadership, but all our members, to come to this place of rest. "Lord, whatever Your will is for my life, I am going to be thankful to You for where You put my hands to labor until You and You alone send me forth. I'm not going to look for the praises of men, even if they totally ignore me on the back side of the hill or the desert. I'm staying right where You put me. And I'll give my life for the sheep as a sacrifice if that is to be the end of me, then that's where I'm going to end it."

You can't miss the will of God with that kind of attitude in the heart. Whatever the future holds, you are open to the will of God. The Sovereign God of the universe can pick you up when He's ready in His perfect timing and put you in the limelight if that is what He wants to do. You don't need to pull, shove, or strive. Just be faithful.

You can't stereotype God's actions. God has a different walk for everyone. His applications are flexible. It wasn't until my father "Ivy" Iverson was fifty-one years old that God placed him in a church as pastor. He had been faithful in serving the house of the Lord for many years. He attended every church meeting. He witnessed faithfully in society. But in 1951, God called this mechanic by trade to begin pastoring what now has become Bible Temple.

What an unlikely prospect in the natural. But God looked on the heart and saw that he would lay a solid foundation for this local church. He and his faithful wife, Sylva, laid an enduring foundation, patiently and thoroughly, for the next generation to build upon.

Four years in a Bible school is simply not an automatic diploma for eldership right after graduation. There are times when God wants to develop a person in other areas of life as well. There is an elder in a local church who spent over twenty years in the armed services. This training exposed him to several lands, and disciplined him into a crew cut, well-ordered individual.

He got saved after all that time, and in a few years felt the call to the ministry. He had spent many years in another occupation. Then in the later years, he was to become an elder. Today, he is one of the most exciting ministers with a large area of responsibility in the local church. His training and discipline have enhanced his present ministry. God in just a few short years turned him into a powerful minister. As for God, His way is perfect. The Word of the Lord is tried and found to be true.

Some song leaders in the local church lead us off into peaceful, quiet-like worship that goes into the heavenlies. That is enjoyable. But it wouldn't be appreciated as much if it were that way all the time. Another elder may have a unique method of leading worship songs that is a powerful type of worship. When he stands us on our feet to sing, we all know we are going to sing. That's great. When things are sort of flat, we all can turn to him to lead us, and things aren't flat for long. But it is God's varied way of training that makes this possible. Do not judge by outward appearance. Expand your horizons and look for potential elders by seeing men as God sees them.

III. EXHORT POTENTIAL ELDERS

An elder is not an organizer, he is a recognizer. One of his responsibilities is to recognize gifts, and talents and ministry in others. With the eyes of the Spirit, he is to see in embryo form the potential for a future minister. And he is not to stop there, but it is vital that he exhort and encourage that embryo to begin the growth process.

A lot of potential ministry has been nipped in the bud because there was not encouraging environment favorable to growth. The seed of potential life-giving ministry has often fallen on stony paths or been trampled upon by unconcerned older ministers in their rush to perform the many other duties in their congregation.

Childhood. No responsible parent would even for one moment consider letting a child grow up "on his own." The parents must have the capacity to recognize abilities and talents in their child and actively encourage him or her to develop those skills. The fact that a parent sees something worth pursuing is very reassuring to the child. Those words of encouragement that are spoken produce a sense of hope and excitement, as well as feelings of worth and acceptance.

So also the church of the living God must not rely upon the volunteer system alone. Potential ministry must be actively and aggressively encouraged.

A word fitly spoken is like apples of gold in pictures of silver. (Proverbs 25:11)

Pleasant words are as an honeycomb, sweet to the soul, and health to the bones. (Proverbs 16:24)

A personal, direct statement of encouragement to a person, does wonders in starting an individual along a field of endeavor. "I would like to see you develop your artistic skills." "You seem to be good in administration. Have you thought of pursuing that field in depth?" "I noticed the keen interest you have in people. Have you thought of teaching?" "Did you write this? Let's see more real soon!" "Keep singing!"

Simple statements of exhortation such as these transform a glowing ember into a flaming passion for fulfillment. They change "I wonder-if doubts" into "affirmations-of-hope." Such confirmations allow the person to respond to the Spirit's dealings already in operation in the deep recesses of the heart.

Everyone has got to where he is today, because someone helped him get there. And it is not just the big scholarships, the gifts or grants, the major endowments or inheritances that transform circumstances or change the destiny of an individual. It is a word spoken at the right time. A compliment given in sincerity. A simple recognition of skill that accomplishes much more than we can imagine in affecting a person's future.

TEAM MINISTRY

Prophecy. The Lord Himself often engages in this important task. In a short prophetic word, He often exposes the deepest desires of the heart of a man and pronounces His confirmation of that desire and sends it along the road of fulfillment. What an impact that prophetic word has! Not simply because that word is from God. But also because the Almighty God of the universe took the time to stop and personally recognize someone's innermost wishes and dreams. And to see the potential resident there in fulfilling those dreams.

Exhortations, either by prophecy or by discernment, are powerful in accomplishing much as far as producing new elders. Blessed by God, they are life-producing words. As elders get older and more tired in body, it is reassuring to know that there are strong, vivacious new elders around to begin shouldering the load of the ministry. It is easier to throw out a well-placed compliment in due season, than for a person to have to do another man's work.

IV. EXAMINE THE MINISTRY

It is mandatory that aspiring elders know the true nature of the ministry. They need to know what the ministry really is. They also need to realize what it is not. It is necessary to comprehend all that the ministry will involve. Jesus admonished us to "count the cost" before embarking on a project (Luke 14:25-33).

The nature of the ministry. As elders training others, we need to show what it really means for an elder to "rule" (Romans 12:8; Hebrews 13:7,17,24; I Timothy 5:17). Ruling, in the Christian sense, is not an ego trip nor simply an opportunity to be in the limelight. It is not an opportunity to seek one's own glory, nor to garner the applause of men (John 5:44; I Thessalonians 2:4; Galatians 1:10). It is not for those who are power hungry (I Peter 5:3).

FORMING THE LEADERSHIP TEAM

So then every one of us shall give account of himself to God.
(Romans 14:12)

But if the watchman see the sword come, and blow not the trumpet...his blood will I require at the watchman's hand. (Ezekiel 33:6)

...they (elders) watch for your souls, as they that must give account...(Hebrews 13:17)

...be not many masters (teachers), knowing that we shall receive the greater condemnation. (James 3:1)

Becoming an elder is a serious undertaking. God will expose the motives of every elder and hold him accountable in the final judgment. And it is sobering to realize that the judgment will be greater.

Ruling. Christ warned his disciples about being true ministers. In the book of Matthew, he compared shepherding to the Pharisees' style (Matthew 23:1-12), and then the Gentile's civil-authority approach (Matthew 20:25-38). The nature of the eldership rule does not allow vainglorious hypocrisy, nor dictatorial manipulation.

The word "rule" in Romans 12:8 is *proistamenoi* and not *archein*. In fact *archein*, to rule in a hierarchial sense, is never used for the Christian ministry. Authority in the church is marked pointedly by the method in which its rulers exercise authority, not so much in the fact of their authority. It is the way in which a ruler is to rule that gives calm assurance to the people in a local church. They are to rule by being an example in life-style. And by ministering the Word through teaching and prophecy.

...Ye know that the princes of the Gentiles exercise dominion over them, and they that are great exercise authority upon them. But it shall not be so among you: but whosoever will be great among you, let him be your minister; and whosoever will be chief among you, let him be your servant: even as the Son of man came...(Matthew 20:25-28)

TEAM MINISTRY

In all things shewing thyself a pattern of good works: in doctrine shewing uncorruptness, gravity, sincerity, sound speech, that cannot be condemned...(Titus 2:7-8)

Feed the flock of God which is among you, taking the oversight thereof, not by constraint, but willingly; not for filthy lucre, but of a ready mind; neither as being lords over God's heritage, but being ensamples to the flock. (I Peter 5:2-3)

...the servant of the Lord must not strive; but be gentle...apt to teach, patient, in meekness instructing those...(II Timothy 2:24-25)

In one word, to rule means serving. An elder is to serve the people. He is to serve even during hardships, even when his labor is unappreciated, even to the point of death, if need be. A new elder must be trained to think in terms of serving, being a slave to the Gospel. It is our duty as elders to teach young men to serve. And to allow God to develop in them a servant's heart.

Paul's life exemplifies the lengths to which a minister must submit if he is to be faithful to his calling:

But in all things approving ourselves as the ministers of God, in much patience, in afflictions, in necessities, in distresses, in stripes, in imprisonments, in tumults, in labours, in watchings, in fastings; by pureness, by knowledge, by longsuffering, by kindness, by the Holy Ghost, by love unfeigned...by honour and dishonour, by evil report and good report: as deceivers, and yet true; as unknown, and yet well known; as dying, and, behold, we live, as chastened, and not killed; as sorrowful, yet always rejoicing; as poor, yet making many rich; as having nothing, and yet possessing all things. (II Corinthians 6:4-6, 8-10)

Are they ministers of Christ?...in labours more abundant, in stripes above measure, in prisons more frequent, in deaths oft. Of the Jews five times received I forty stripes save one. Thrice was I beaten with rods, once was I stoned, thrice I suffered shipwreck, a night and a day I have been in the deep; in journeyings often, in perils of waters, in perils of robbers, in perils by mine own countrymen, in perils by the heathen, in perils in the city, in perils in the wilderness, in perils in the sea, in perils among false brethren; in weariness and painfulness, in watchings often, in hunger and thirst, in fastings often, in cold and

FORMING THE LEADERSHIP TEAM

nakedness. Beside those things that are without, that which cometh upon me daily, the care of all the churches. (II Corinthians 11:23-28)

Paul talked about being "pressed out of measure, above strength" (II Corinthians 1:8-9), of endless days working day and night (I Thessalonians 2:1-13), of rejection by his friends (II Timothy 1:15), mental exhaustion (II Corinthians 4:8-10), and physical scars (Galatians 6:17). All of these were a part of the glorious ministry.

Now, there are certainly highlights and joys connected with ministering. But new elders must realize that rewards are mainly reserved for the end of life's work. Now is a time of service. This is the clear teaching of Jesus (Mark 10:44; Luke 12:37; John 12:24-26). It is to be the prime motivation of each elder. This teaching will send new elders on the way to maturity.

V. EXPLAIN THE DEALINGS OF GOD

Potential elders will hasten in their maturity if they understand how God deals with an individual through circumstances. As elders, we are wise if we explain this to them, and then have the patience to step back periodically and let God allow circumstances "to stretch" them. There are many talented and skilled young men in the world and in the church. There are many of high academic caliber and intelligence. But there men are disqualified for ministry if their character does not come up to the level of their talent. The total man must be developed before he is to be thrust into the ministry as an elder. A man's character must come up to the level of his gift and skills.

A mature character. Maturity of character exhibits three basic qualities: a heart after God, a heart devoted to service toward man, and, a heart of integrity within himself. Failure in any one of these can spell doom and

TEAM MINISTRY

shipwreck in the ministry of leadership. God considers them so important that in His sovereignty He uses circumstances to develop and enhance them.

Solitude. The first kind of circumstance God uses is solitude. God at times chooses to place potential elders in isolation, solitary places, alone. John the Baptist was "in the desert" until the time of his showing to Israel (Luke 1:80). The Apostle Paul spent a little while in Arabia and Damascus getting his life in order after his conversion (Galatians 1:17). Moses lived in the isolated Midian desert for many years before his showing to Israel and Egypt (Exodus 3). King David spent his younger years on the backside of the wilderness tending sheep (I Samuel 16:11).

Because of an emptiness inside, a spiritual void, many people cannot stand to be alone. To them, silence is deafening. They can't live with themselves, so they fill the airwaves with noise. They must constantly have the stereo on full blast, or listen to the television, or fly high on the latest radio disco beat.

The atmosphere of solitude ministers to our spirits. Many run from this time of quiet. Yet, the solitary atmosphere is an opportunity to deepen our spiritual maturity. It is a time to be alone with God.

Obscurity. Another circumstance God often uses to bring out true grit is obscurity. He sometimes puts us out where no one can see our great heroic adventures. A man who truly has a servant's heart does not serve because he is seen.

...but do not ye after their works (Pharisees)...all their works they do for to be seen of men...(Matthew 23:3,5)

How can ye believe, which receive honour one of another, and seek not the honour that cometh from God only? (John 5:44)

FORMING THE LEADERSHIP TEAM

Servants, be obedient...not with eyeservice, as menpleasers; but as the servants of Christ, doing the will of God from the heart. (Ephesians 6:5-6)

When people are looking, a person can be "oh so very diligent." But service in public does not necessarily reflect a servant's heart. However, when one is in a place of obscurity, where nobody knows what you are doing, yet you are giving, serving and pouring out your life and strength and time, then you are developing a true servant's heart.

As a marriage counselor, it is strongly advisable to discourage couples from marrying too young. The reason for this is that it is too hard to nurture "under prying eyes." It is hard for a man to grow with a wife watching him. Pride and the male ego are very strong factors.

So also with young elders. It is easier to mature and develop in obscurity. It is not so easy after you've been placed in a leadership role, with dozens of people watching you. The growth process tends to stop in immaturely placed young men, and a defensive spirit takes over. Potential elders must take full advantage of the circumstance of obscurity that God has placed them in for proper maturation. God knows where you are. Obscurity is not synonymous with neglect. God is not neglecting a young elder at such a time. On the contrary, He is hard at work molding character in him.

Monotony. The third place or circumstance that God uses to develop character is in a place of monotony. Anyone can hang around when there is revival excitement in the air. But few care to stick around after the party and do the clean up. Being faithful in the menial, insignificant, routine, regular, unexciting, uneventful, mundane, unthankful tasks is part of the training of the man of God.

In little things, we prove ourselves capable of bigger

TEAM MINISTRY

things. What you do now. What sacrifices you make now. These are important to God. God isn't waiting for your heyday. This is your day. Today is your day. And the question He asks is "What are you doing with today?"

> He that is faithful in that which is least is faithful also in much: and he that is unjust in the least is unjust also in the much. If therefore ye have not been faithful in the unrighteous mammon, who will commit to your trust the true riches? And if ye have not been faithful in that which is another man's, who shall give you that which is your own? (Luke 16:10-12)
>
> His lord said unto him, Well done, thou good and faithful servant: thou hast been faithful over a few things, I will make thee ruler over many things: enter thou into the joy of thy lord. (Matthew 25:21)
>
> As the cold of snow in the time of harvest, so is a faithful messenger to them that send him: for he refresheth the soul of his masters. (Proverbs 25:13)
>
> Confidence in an unfaithful man in time of trouble is like a broken tooth, and a foot out of joint. (Proverbs 25:19)

This principle of faithfulness in the monotonous things of life is found throughout the entire Bible. The reason God blessed and worked through men in the past is because He found them to be faithful: Abraham (Galatians 3:9), Moses (Numbers 12:7), David (I Samuel 22:14), Daniel (Daniel 6:3-4), Paul (I Timothy 1:12), Timothy (I Corinthians 4:17), and Tychicus (Ephesians 6:21).

Teach young elders not to minimize the situation in which they presently find themselves. They are to be diligent at what their hands find to do. Don't make comparisons of present circumstances with someone else's state of affairs. "It's not what you've got. It's what you do with what you've got!" That's what counts with God. If you are faithful at where God has placed you, then He is always at work on your behalf. Let this message ring out loud and clear to all potential elders.

FORMING THE LEADERSHIP TEAM

God uses these various circumstances--solitude, obscurity and monotony--to stretch young men and build character in them. It is a process that must go on in their lives. People often shy away from these circumstances and that's why they miss the will of God. They don't develop spiritually, because it's in these areas that the grit of character and spirituality are fostered. God's choice of methods and God's ways are contrary to human reasoning and man's methods. But remember, God is constantly looking at the heart of man.

God is never in a hurry in developing inner qualities. Going through these circumstances takes time, but if you let Him mold you this way you will come out as pure gold. An elder's ministry is dependent upon his heart condition. Don't worry about promotion. God will pull the young elder from the desert place and put him in the limelight when the timing is right.

VI. EXPEND ENERGY

Each new elder has a unique and specific ministry, ordained by the Lord in which he is to function. Along with that role of service to the body, the Lord provides certain gifts for the potential elder in order to facilitate the fulfillment of that role. Often these gifts are given during the laying-on-of-hands service, or ordination, or by a prophetic ministry.

It needs to be kept in mind though, that the gifts and challenges of God do not come to pass without any human effort. They do not find fulfillment spontaneously. Several passages in the Bible address this issue:

And say to Archippus, Take heed to the ministry which thou hast received in the Lord, that thou fulfil it. (Colossians 4:17)

Neglect not the gift that is in thee, which was given thee by prophecy, with the laying on of the hands of the presbytery. Meditate upon these things; give thyself wholly to them; that thy profiting may appear to all. (I Timothy 4:14-15)

TEAM MINISTRY

Wherefore I put thee in remembrance that thou stir up the gift of God, which is in thee by the putting on of my hands. For God hath not given us the spirit of fear...(II Timothy 1:6-7)

For God is not unrighteous to forget your work and labour of love...in that ye have ministered to the saints, and do minister. And we desire that every one of you do shew the same diligence to the full assurance of hope to the end: that ye be not slothful...(Hebrews 6:10-12)

The hand of the diligent shall bear rule: but the slothful shall be under tribute. (Proverbs 12:24)

Wherefore the rather, brethren, give diligence to make your calling and election sure: for if ye do these things, ye shall never fall. (II Peter 1:10)

For many are called, but few are chosen. (Matthew 22:14; see also 20:16)

While the ministry is a spiritual ministry and therefore supernatural, the Bible indicates that there is a very real practical work involved in applying it to everyday life. There is an inherent danger of thinking that because the presbytery has decreed through prophecy that someone is going to be an apostle, evangelist, or whatever, that he can now sit back and watch it happen.

It is easy to dig out the transcript of a prophecy, read it and then say, "Well God, I'm waiting; here I am, do your thing." Then a year later, "Hey God, I thought you said I was going to be an apostle. How come nothing is happening?" A sort of pagan fatalism sets into our thinking. "What will be, will be."

However, the Word says that once we know God's direction and will for our lives in serving the body, we then are to set our face like a flint and with unswerving dedication and singleness of purpose, prepare to the best of our ability for the accomplishing of that will.

A prospective elder must not be sidetracked by carnal allurements such as covetousness in moneymaking schemes and investments:

FORMING THE LEADERSHIP TEAM

Moreover thou shalt provide out of all the people able men, such as fear God, men of truth, hating covetousness; and place such over them, to be rulers...(Exodus 18:21)

These and other entanglements drain time and energy from the preparation for the ministry:

Thou therefore endure hardness, as a good solider of Jesus Christ. No man that warreth entangleth himself with the affairs of this life; that he may please Him who hath chosen him to be a soldier. (II Timothy 2:3-4)

Paul even suggested that a person remain single if marriage would distract too much from serving the Lord (I Corinthians 7:32). That may be a little too much for some, and it is certainly only for those who can bear it (Matthew 19:11). But the point is well taken. Diligence must be exercised in not steering away from the prize of the high calling in Christ (Philippians 3:13-14). Nothing must be allowed to detract from preparing for the ministry. We were given some insight into Nehemiah's success when he stated:

Yea, also I continued in the work of this wall, neither bought we any land: and all my servants were gathered thither unto the work. (Nehemiah 5:16)

His whole concentration of thought and effort was given to the important task at hand. Neither farm investments, nor monetary enticements, nor compromising treaties deterred him from doing the Lord's work.

If a young elder's creativity wanes, his morale sags; or if he lacks proper motivation, or is slack in faithfulness, it is time to check his priorities. What remorse, what weeping and wailing there might be for someone to look back from the shores of eternity toward the life spent on earth and wonder if perhaps it had been wasted, frittered

TEAM MINISTRY

away on trivials. And all for what? What can compare to the prize of the high calling in Christ:

> *For I reckon that the sufferings of this present time are not worthy to be compared with the glory which shall be revealed in us. (Romans 8:18)*

Operation of gifts. As was stated before, God often gives supernatural gifts to an individual to help him function in his appointed role. It is yet to be recorded that a person moved in his gift perfectly when he first received it. A pastor recently remarked that when he began moving in the gift of healing, he had a twenty percent success rate. Now it is up to eighty to eighty-five percent. He has had to wait on God, research the Word, and go through tests of faith to develop this gift that God has given him. He has gone through times of discouragement when someone dies instead of getting healed. And today, there are still some things about his gift that he doesn't understand. But he is diligent to press on in obedient faith to develop his ministry. And that's the way it is in the exercise of all gifts.

There are steps of faith in developing ministry. A young up-and-coming elder must expend some energy in long hard hours of contemplation, research, prayer and fasting in the area of his calling. The prophetic word that has been given over a person must be proven in practice:

> *Despise not prophesyings. Prove all things; hold fast that which is good. (I Thessalonians 5:20-21)*

> *But let every man prove his own work, and then shall he have rejoicing in himself alone, and not in another. (Galatians 6:4)*

> *And we have sent them with our brother, whom we have oftentimes proved diligent in many things...(II Corinthians 8:22)*

A young elder-to-be needs to be taught not to despise the day of small beginnings. He has to start somewhere in the exercise of his gift. But if he waits for the day of perfection before he can exercise it, the opportunity for ministry may pass him by.

Teaching ability. While various and sundry gifts are given to different elders by the Lord for the carrying out of the ministry of ruling as an elder, there is one aspect of the ministry that every elder must diligently develop: the ability to teach the Word, and to handle the Word skillfully.

> *Remember them which have the rule over you, who have spoken unto you the Word of God...(Hebrews 13:7)*
>
> *A bishop (overseer) then must be...apt to teach. (I Timothy 3:2)*
>
> *Take heed therefore unto yourselves, and to all the flock, over the which the Holy Ghost hath made you overseers, to feed the church of God...(Acts 20:28)*
>
> *For a bishop (overseer) must be blameless...holding fast the faithful word as he hath been taught, that he may be able by sound doctrine both to exhort and to convince the gainsayers. (Titus 1:7-9)*

The thing that separates an ordinary elder from a good elder is the amount of diligence and energy spent in studying and understanding the Word. The authority of an elder is based upon the ability to know and communicate "thus saith the Lord." Ruling has to do with "feeding" the life-giving Word to sheep who hunger after righteousness. As soon as an elder stops feeding, for all intents and purposes, he stops ruling.

As a parent, if one just lays around on the couch and watches television and reads comic books, what authority do you think he will have with his children? He may order them around, tell them to do this and that. But if he's not putting any food on the table, nor feeding their spirits with right attitudes and precepts, then there's going to be a rebellion in that household. In the natural, a father's authority isn't just because he's a man and he knows how to shout. Brute strength may for a while be able to enforce tranquility at home, but respect for authority has probably dissipated long ago.

It is similar in the house of God. You can place people in positions of ruling over the church and given them titles. But if these leaders aren't feeding and nourishing God's people then they aren't legitimate overseers.

When the Apostle Paul listed the requirements for elders, and then for deacons (I Timothy 3:1-13), he gave basically only one additional requirement for the elders: that they know how to teach. The ruling ministers must substantiate their authority by anointed teaching.

The skill of teaching and holding forth the Word of Life is produced first by knowing the Author of the Book. His Holy Spirit is the inspiration of the Book and its best interpreter as well. An elder cannot understand the ways of God without knowing God himself. He must teach young men to pray through a passage.

Then an understanding of the Word can be obtained by attending a good Bible-believing Bible college. It is good to survey the entire Bible; learn the cultural, economic, geographic, and political settings and background; study the original languages in which it was written; and delve into expository research.

An elder should also enhance his handling of the Word by developing his own personal library. There are many inexpensive reference works and available commentaries. Young elders should "pick the brains" of old warriors in the faith. Find out which books have influenced their ministries for good.

> *Study to shew thyself approved unto God, a workman that needeth not to be ashamed, rightly dividing the Word of truth.* (II Timothy 2:15)

> *Take heed unto thyself, and unto the doctrine; continue in them: for in doing this thou shalt both save thyself, and them that hear thee.* (I Timothy 4:16)

FORMING THE LEADERSHIP TEAM

In all areas of the ministry, a potential elder must diligently apply himself to skillfully serve the Lord's people. He must teach them above all not to neglect the handling of the life-giving Word.

In the ancient synagogues, three elders were necessary to be present during the performance of the service, and one of the three had to be a skilled teacher.

When the apostles were alive, the early church relied on them to teach all the doctrines they had heard from the lips of Christ. But with the passing away of the apostles, the rise of good and faithful teachers became crucial. The doctrine had to remain pure. There were pressures from Judaizers to compromise the Gospel with the Law. There were occult cults that wanted to get in on the supernatural secrets. And there were vain philosophers that were eager to fit this new doctrine into their mind set. These dangers still plague the church today.

> And the things that thou hast heard of me among many witnesses, the same commit thou to faithful men, who shall be able to teach others also. (II Timothy 2:2)

The admonition of Paul to Timothy is just as critically important today as it was then. Young elders must expend energy in this area of ministry.

VII. EXPECT FLAWS AND FAILURES

The closer a person comes under scrutiny, the more imperfections will be seen. In training prospective elders you are going to see several character flaws and personality weaknesses. God is going to be dealing with these. He is going to allow circumstances, adversities, and sometimes tragedies to cross the paths of the individual to purge him.

> Every branch in Me that beareth not fruit He taketh away: and ever branch that beareth fruit, He purgeth it, that it may bring forth more fruit. (John 15:2)

TEAM MINISTRY

The word for purge in this passage is the Greek word from which we derive "catharsis." It means a cleansing, a getting rid of disease that might hurt the fruit. Sometimes aspiring elders, who are producing fruit, still need to go through a major emotional and spiritual catharsis. God is interested in the fruit remaining. He finds it necessary sometimes to cleanse away even the slightest character quirks and flaws.

As pastors and elders we need to realize this. We need to realize what is going on. Often we are in a hurry to take a young man who shows promise, and place him in a position of leadership, and take advantage of his talents and skills. Then suddenly the "bottom drops out." The one whom we thought was perfect for the job is now coming apart at the seams! We need to realize that God is not rejecting him, nor were we wrong in diagnosing potential in him. But there is a cleansing process that must go on in those who are totally dedicated to becoming ministers of the Most High.

Sometimes we panic and try to patch things up too soon, not realizing that God is at work. We hinder the Word of God in that person. It is hard to stand back and realize that he must go through it. None of us likes to see our children suffer or fail. But it is these times that are the greatest learning experiences in a Christian's life. It is these times when the greatest growth is made possible. Listen to the wisdom of the Bible:

> *It is good for me that I have been afflicted; that I might learn Thy statutes...They that fear Thee will be glad when they see me; because I have hoped in Thy Word. I know, O Lord, that Thy judgments are right, and that Thou in faithfulness hast afflicted me. (Psalm 119:71, 74-75)*

> *It is good for a man that he bear the yoke in his youth. He sitteth alone and keepeth silence, because He hath borne it upon him. He putteth his mouth in the dust; if so be there may be hope. He giveth his cheek to Him that smiteth him: he is filled full with reproach.*

FORMING THE LEADERSHIP TEAM

For the Lord will not cast off for ever: But though He cause grief, yet will He have compassion according to the multitude of His mercies. For He doth not afflict willingly nor grieve the children of men. (Lamentations 3:27-33)

...My son, despise not thou the chastening of the Lord, nor faint when thou art rebuked of Him: for whom the Lord loveth He chasteneth, and scourgeth every son whom He receiveth. If ye endure chastening, God dealeth with you as with sons...But if ye be without chastisement, whereof all are partakers, then are ye bastards, and not sons...He (chasteneth) for our profit, that we might be partakers of His holiness. (Hebrews 12:5-10; see also Proverbs 3:11)

Most of the great men of the Bible went through the valleys of testing and chastisement. David was abused by Saul. Elijah went through great periods of discouragement. Abraham had to go to Mount Moriah. Moses fell flat on his face as a young man in Egypt's courts. Joseph had to be humbled in prison. And Jacob had to wrestle with a higher power and be afflicted.

These experiences take time, sometimes several years! You have to let them go through it. You must let them fail. Some men have to be pushed to the extreme. The work of cleansing must be thorough. When steel is tempered, it is put through a heat treatment. When gold is refined it experiences the heat:

Who are kept by the power of God through faith unto salvation ready to be revealed in the last time. Wherein ye greatly rejoice, though now for a season, if need be ye are in heaviness through manifold temptations: that the trial of your faith, being much more precious than of gold that perisheth, though it be tried with fire, might be found unto praise and honor and glory at the appearing of Jesus Christ. (I Peter 1:5-7)

During these times, the wise realize that God alone is their strength. That the Lord is their Shepherd. Scales drop from their eyes. They see the love and glory of God in greater dimensions. The wisdom and sovereignty of

TEAM MINISTRY

God becomes more meaningful. His laws and precepts shine more brightly in splendor. Their hearts are enlarged and that is the crux of the matter.

While we cannot interfere with the dealings of God in an individual's life, we, as elders, are required to encourage those who are going through it. The passage in the book of Hebrews dealing with discipline (chapter 12) includes an admonition to "lift up the hands which hang down." There is a quotation in Isaiah worth considering:

The wilderness and the solitary place shall be glad for them; and the desert shall rejoice, and blossom as the rose. It shall blossom abundantly, and rejoice even with joy and singing...they shall see the glory of the Lord, and the excellency of our God. (Isaiah 35:1,2)

Strengthen ye the weak hands, and confirm the feeble knees. Say to them that are of a fearful heart, Be strong, fear not: behold, your God will come with vengeance, even God with recompense; he will come and save you. (Isaiah 35:3,4)

Then the eyes of the blind shall be opened, and the ears of the deaf shall be unstopped. Then shall the lame man leap as an hart, and the tongue of the dumb sing...(Isaiah 35:5,6)

And the ransomed of the Lord shall return, and come to Zion with songs and everlasting joy upon their heads: they shall obtain joy and gladness, and sorrow and sighing shall flee away. (Isaiah 35:10)

Hope must be placed before the discouraged person. The testing is for good. The testing is not only "salvation" for the man of God. The results of the purging also will be an enablement to open the eyes of the blind, and heal the sick. Weeping endures but for the night. Joy comes in the morning.

Expect times of trial in the lives of potential elders. Let them go through it. Also be a point of reference so they don't feel totally lost. Be an encouragement. Present hope to them of Christ's faithfulness.

FORMING THE LEADERSHIP TEAM

VIII. EXPOSE MEN TO SERVICE

Aspiring elders must be exposed to opportunities of service if they are to fully mature. Assign young men to obscure jobs both in the church and in the community. Keep tabs on how they respond to the monotonous chores and everyday routines. Teach faithfulness in the little things by making sure they have opportunities to serve "the least in the kingdom." The "young men" (Acts 5:6,10) should be volunteering to teach Sunday school classes, to maintain the church building and grounds, to mow the lawns of the poor and elderly, and to assist those struck by tragedy. Jesus went about doing good, and the servant is not above the master (Matthew 10:24).

In time, it is wise also for an experienced elder to take a prospective elder under his wing. Let him observe how he ministers in the church. Jesus chose twelve to be "with him" so that they in turn might know how to guide the church (Mark 3:14). Timothy was with Paul (Acts 16:3) and was instructed by the Apostle on how to rule the churches. In the Old Testament Joshua assisted Moses. Elisha poured water on the hands of Elijah. Hanani helped Nehemiah.

On-site apprenticeship is a valuable learning method. Young men ought to accompany elders on their hospital visits, emergency responses and evangelism calls. They should travel with them to speaking engagements, when they are teaching seminars, and when they are preaching in jails and missions. If a young man feels that God has given him a prophetic gift, he should latch on to one of the prophetic elders. A prospective teacher should get acquainted with the personal library of the teaching elder when possible.

Elders are not to be domineering, but helpers (II Corinthians 1:24). They are to reproduce themselves in the younger generation. Just as Christ left us examples by

TEAM MINISTRY

actual practice and deeds, so ministers must train new elders by example.

Christ also suffered for us, leaving us an example, that ye should follow His steps. (I Peter 2:21)

Brethren, be followers together of me, and mark them which walk so as ye have us for an ensample. (Philippians 3:17)

Be ye followers of me, even as I also am of Christ. (I Corinthians 11:1)

The word for "follow" is the Greek word from which we get "mime." By following the young elder is miming, or acting out by duplication, those things shown and taught by the experienced minister. Older ministers must invest time, take time to be with the aspiring young men. That takes patience.

Each new generation in the church needs well trained leadership to carry on the important ministry to the body. This is best facilitated by unlearned men serving alongside experienced elders. Just to watch and listen to your elder in action is of great benefit. To watch him respond to different situations is enlightening.

Another way for aspiring elders to learn by doing is in "home meetings" or "home Bible study groups." Many churches have divided their congregations into "district" and/or "home" meetings which gather on a regular basis. This is a tremendous opportunity for potential elders to flex their teaching and exhorting muscles. It is a great time to learn to pray for the sick, and bring deliverance to those in bondage.

Inspiration without expression leads to frustration. If a person feels a call to the fivefold ministry, but has no opportunity to work out and develop that call in a practical way, he may end up frustrated and eventually bitter. Encourage the young men to communicate with their elders. The young men need to be reminded occasionally that they can and are to come to the elders for guidance in developing their ministry, because the elders are there to help them.

Promotion is something else. It is God who promotes in His timing. But it is the elders' responsibility to develop, train and provide opportunities of service for the young man. Guidance counselling before a bitterness crisis solidifies is a lot easier to handle than crisis counselling after the fact. Elders have busy schedules. They may be hard pressed to take time out from their other duties. But it shows initiative (one of the ingredients of a good leader) when a person hangs on to an elder and says, "I will not let you go, till you bless me!"

One idea that has been a blessing for aspiring leaders is the formation of a fellowship of young people preparing for the ministry. In one city nearly three hundred meet every month for dinner, testimonies and reports on the development of the members of the group in their reaching a field of service. What an encouragement it is for each to share ideas, problems and possible solutions in training for the ministry.

In some cities, all the pastors get together for fellowship on a monthly basis. It would be extremely beneficial if occasionally they opened up their fellowship to the aspiring ministry, the potential elders, and share their experiences with them. Potential elders might be saved such heartbreak by the wisdom of the older ministry. Exposure to the experiences of others in their service in the church will help develop the young men.

IX. EXUDE CONFIDENCE

The church is the Lord's. Exude the confidence and faith that He will watch over it. And He will assist in developing new ministries to provide a continuity from generation to generation.

TEAM MINISTRY

...Be strong and of good courage, and do it: fear not, nor be dismayed: for the Lord God, even my God, will be with thee; He will not fail thee, nor forsake thee, until thou hast finished all the work for the service of the house of the Lord. (I Chronicles 28:20)

Sometimes even when we overlook and neglect a potential elder, it is because God has blinded our eyes so that He may deal directly with that individual. He is the Good Shepherd. He desires that eventually all young men are weaned away from their earthly elders and that they follow the One who is the Bishop of their souls. He, and He alone, is "the hope of glory" both in this life and in the one to come.

...Christ in you, the hope of glory: Whom we preach, warning every man, and teaching every man in all wisdom; that we may present every man perfect (mature) in Christ Jesus. (Colossians 1:27-28)